MOUNTAIN MYTH

Also by Terrell T. Garren

THE SECRET OF WAR
*A Dramatic History of Civil War Crime
in Western North Carolina*

MOUNTAIN MYTH

Unionism in Western North Carolina

Terrell T. Garren

THE REPRINT COMPANY, PUBLISHERS
Spartanburg, South Carolina
2006

Copyright © 2006 Terrell T. Garren
All rights reserved

An original publication, 2006
THE REPRINT COMPANY, PUBLISHERS
Spartanburg, South Carolina 29304

ISBN-10: 0-87152-552-6
ISBN-13: 978-0-87152-552-9
Library of Congress Control Number 2006934426
Manufactured in the United States of America

∞

The paper used in this publication meets the minimum requirements
of American National Standard for Information Sciences—Permanence
of Paper for Printed Library Materials, ANSI Z39.48-1984

Contents

PREFACE
vii

ACKNOWLEDGMENTS
ix

CHAPTER ONE
Unionism | *1*

CHAPTER TWO
Alexander Hamilton Jones | *6*

CHAPTER THREE
Union Troops from Western North Carolina | *15*

CHAPTER FOUR
Confederate Troops from Western North Carolina | *84*

CHAPTER FIVE
Slavery | *112*

CHAPTER SIX
The Monuments | *115*

CHAPTER SEVEN
The Anti-Confederates | *135*

CHAPTER EIGHT
African-Americans | *141*

CHAPTER NINE
The Aftermath | *144*

BIBLIOGRAPHY
153

INDEX
157

Preface

Beginning in 1989 I became engaged in a long-term research project that led to my first novel, which was set in western North Carolina during the Civil War period. The novel was based on the true-life experience of my great-grandmother, Delia Russell Youngblood. In writing that book a sincere effort was made to keep the fictionalized account in line with documented history whenever possible.

In order to meet a higher standard of historical accuracy and compatibility with the official record a great deal of research had to be completed. After spending more than a decade and a half on this effort I have compiled a significant collection of historical documents and information pertaining to the topic. As a result, my interest in a nonfiction study involving my research has emerged. *Mountain Myth* is a product of that interest.

The reader is advised that the author has no educational credentials as an historian.

My educational credentials are in the fields of education and public school administration. It is my personal opinion that such a study initiated by someone from outside the academic mainstream does offer some advantage. There are also obvious disadvantages that the reader should consider.

This history will be presented for what it is, an interpretation of the period by the author. I recognize that there are conflicting views regarding some of my hypotheses, and I will try to present alternative theories and opinions within the text whenever possible. The reader is also advised that even though this topic involves something that happened nearly a century and a half ago, new information continues to emerge. Future historians may unearth information or documents that add to this story at a later date.

In the course of researching my novel *The Secret of War*, I made a significant discovery that conflicted with previous historical interpretations. The story of Unionism in our region has been substantially misunderstood and exaggerated. It is my hope that this work will shed new light on an old topic for the benefit of the reader and future historians.

Acknowledgments

I would like to express my sincere appreciation to Dr. Richard Sommers and the staff at the U.S. Army Military History Institute. Dr. Sommers was both challenging and inspiring in his efforts to encourage me to seek an accurate understanding of the records and the history.

I would also like to offer a special thanks to the staff at Pack Memorial Library in Asheville, North Carolina. During the many days in the library I spent reading twenty-seven thousand Confederate troops records, they were always courteous and helpful in every way.

Mr. Chris Mecons at the North Carolina Office of Archives and History was very helpful along with his colleague Mr. Mike Hill. The staff at the Tennessee State Archives in Nashville, Tennessee, were also helpful.

Throughout the many years I've worked on Civil War research projects I could always count on the Henderson County Genealogical and Historical Society for resources and help. In recent years the Old Buncombe County Genealogical Society has provided the same support. I thank the societies, their staffs, and their members for their assistance.

The new National Archives facility in Morrow, Georgia, is greatly appreciated. The staff was helpful and knowledgeable.

A special thanks to Trena Parker, Solari Garren, Rachel Staley, Jasmine Kimmel, and Phyllis Corley, who all helped in some way. I also thank

Susan Snowden, of Snowden Editorial Services, for the excellent work she did in editing this book.

Most of all, I offer my deepest gratitude to my wife, Maria Glass Garren. A descendant of a mountain Union soldier, she is my conscience and my inspiration. I thank her for her sacrifice and her patience.

Chapter One

—— UNIONISM ——

On April 10, 1865, famed Confederate General Robert E. Lee became a Unionist. He put forth the word and called for all Southerners to lay down their arms and embrace the Union and reconciliation. Within a couple of months practically all Confederate forces in the field had surrendered, and tens of thousands of Confederate soldiers had taken the oath of allegiance to the flag of their former enemy. Should history describe Lee and his men as Unionists? Some men have been so described in western North Carolina history works with less supporting evidence than would be required to classify Lee as such.

It has been demonstrated that the word "Unionism" has different meanings to different people. How one defines the term is a critical part of any evaluation.

Definitions of a Unionist are as follows:
1. An individual from a Confederate state who remained loyal to the Union during the American Civil War.
2. An individual who served in the Union army at some time during the war.
3. An individual or family who refused to support the Confederacy. This definition would include deserters and conscription evaders.

4. Any individual with a U.S. shield on his gravestone.
5. Any individual or family who claimed to be Unionist after the war was over.
6. Anyone who became a Republican after the war.
7. Anyone who moved to western North Carolina after the war who had some previous Union affiliation.
8. One who adheres to the policy of a firm Federal union between the states of the United States, especially during the Civil War period.[1]

One may choose to accept any of these definitions. The desire to label as many people as possible as "Unionist" has led to incorrect inclusions and misinterpretation of the evidence.

To the outsider observing this debate it may seem that there was "substantial" or "considerable" Unionism in western North Carolina at the time of the Civil War. Our history is often presented in a way that gives the impression to an outside observer that western North Carolina was significantly different than the rest of the South in this regard. The causes for this misleading impression are many, but the use of any and all of the definitions previously listed are at the root of the issue. In order to fully evaluate the issue one must ask the questions: What did they do? And when did they do it? General Lee and his men came over to the Union in the end but it would be grossly inaccurate to describe them as Unionists. Timing is everything when one attempts to judge Unionism in western North Carolina.

At least partial answers to those questions can be found in the records. The most difficult question to answer is: Why did they do it?

It is the opinion of the author that acceptance of various loose definitions mislead the reader or listener. The outsider is given the false impression that the war started and families immediately chose sides and that many chose the Union. I estimate that in late 1861 or early 1862 less than 5 percent of the people of our region were Unionist, as defined by definition number one or eight. Very few of the men from WNC who went over to the Federal army did so before the battle of Gettysburg in 1863.

It is often represented that there were certain counties that were Union and some that were Confederate at the beginning of the war. It is likely that almost everyone in western North Carolina became a Confederate after Fort Sumter and Lincoln's call for troops to invade the South. The emotional frenzy that followed these events might be compared to citizen reaction to the bombing of Pearl Harbor at the beginning of World War II. While the number of people who supported secession prior to Fort Sumter was probably around 30 percent, that percentage leaped to a level that was close to or exceeding 95 percent afterward. Such description applies accurately to all western North Carolina counties.

In sixteen years of study I have come to understand that only definitions number one and eight accurately represent a Unionist. In western North Carolina during the Civil War, some local men went into the Union army during the latter part of the war. One must fully examine the timing and motivations of these men to get a full understanding of the issue. True mountain Unionists would have been a rare thing in the fall of 1861.

While Unionism certainly existed, the mythology is a result of exaggeration. A Federal uniform may seem to indicate true loyalty to the Union, but it might really represent something else. In any state of the Union and in most countries, a contract obtained under duress is not legal. Approximately one-fifth of the men who went into the Union army did so to escape torture and death in a Union prison. Several thousand Western North Carolina Confederates were captured during the war. Some joined the enemy; thousands refused. As a result there are 976 documented cases of western North Carolina Confederates who died in Union prisons.[2]

What areas are considered to be part of western North Carolina?

As is the case with the term "unionism," western North Carolina can have different meanings to different people. The state has been traditionally divided into three geographic areas: coastal, the piedmont and the mountains. For the purposes of this study of Unionism during the Civil War a more specific definition has been established.

It seems most appropriate to accept a definition used by a man who should be referred to as the father of the Unionism myth. His name was Alexander Hamilton Jones. A full chapter will be devoted to Jones later in this book but for now we will outline only his description of western North Carolina.

Jones wrote his campaign autobiography in 1866 while attempting to gain a seat in the United States House of Representatives. He was not seated initially because North Carolina had not been readmitted to the Union. Therefore, Jones appropriately named his self-promotional autobiography *Knocking at the Door.*

Jones defined western North Carolina as consisting of the twenty most western counties plus Wilkes County.[3] It is important to remember that Graham, Swain, and Avery counties did not exist at the time. Graham was part of Cherokee and Macon counties. Swain was part of Jackson and Macon counties. Avery County was part of several surrounding counties.

For the purposes of this study the counties included are as follows:
1. ASHE
2. BUNCOMBE
3. BURKE
4. CALDWELL
5. CATAWBA
6. CHEROKEE
7. CLAY

8. CLEVELAND
9. HAYWOOD
10. HENDERSON
11. JACKSON
12. MACON
13. MADISON
14. MCDOWELL
15. MITCHELL
16. POLK
17. RUTHERFORD
18. TRANSYLVANIA
19. WATAUGA
20. WILKES
21. YANCEY

Scholars of western North Carolina Civil War history have often referred to certain counties as being more Union than other counties. Wilkes County may have had more Unionists than Cleveland County, for example, but that does not necessarily mean that Wilkes County was a Union county. It is probable that every county in every Confederate state had some Unionism but that doesn't necessarily define those counties as Unionist. Such identity is often associated with East Tennessee and correctly so, but circumstances and attitudes were quite different in the mountains of North Carolina.

REFERENCES
1. *Merriam-Webster's Collegiate Dictionary*, 11th ed., s.v. "unionism."
2. Jordan, Weymouth T., and Louis H. Manarin, *North Carolina Troops, 1861-1865: A Roster*. North Carolina Office of Archives and History, Department of Cultural Resources, 1966.
3. Jones, A. H., *Knocking at the Door*, McGill & Witherow, Printers and Stereotypers, Washington, D.C., 1866, page 35.

Chapter Two

—— ALEXANDER HAMILTON JONES ——

In his book *Knocking at the Door* Alexander Hamilton Jones represents himself as being totally loyal to the Union from the beginning. The book was used as his campaign autobiography promoting his attempt to gain a seat in Congress. He recounts being conscripted, arrested, and confined at Castle Thunder Prison in Richmond, Virginia, by Confederate authorities.

The most consistent message contained in the thirty-eight page work is that Jones is a true Union man. While I believe Jones exaggerated his claims about Unionism, one must consider the unusual nature of the 1866 campaign for Congress in western North Carolina. The region was under military occupation. The Union army was in charge of everything including the election.

Alexander Hamilton Jones realized something that many others may not have recognized at the time. The best path to winning that election was to be the "Union man." He saw the opportunity and seized it. Jones won the 1866 election but he was not seated because North Carolina had not been officially readmitted to the Union.

I am not the first, nor will I be the last, to question the claims made in Jones's book. In most cases an individual's claims don't mean much to historians. In this case the statements are critical because Jones is the primary source cited for Union troop counts from western North Carolina during the Civil War. On page thirty-five Jones writes:

"From actual calculation it is ascertained that from the twenty counties comprising the mountain or seventh congressional district of North Carolina, with the additional county of Wilkes, no less than five thousand seven hundred and ninety white males from the age of seventeen years and upwards, crossed the lines; three-fourths of which number were in the Federal army, besides one hundred and eighty-three who it is known lost their lives in the effort to get through."[1]

Many good historians have done a lot of great work over the years since Jones published his campaign biography. Many of these writers have included estimates of men from western North Carolina who were in the Union army. Readers often assume that these authors have attempted to estimate the number on their own. The reality is that most of them may have relied on the same source: A. H. Jones's *Knocking at the Door.*

There is good reason why most of these writers and historians did not attempt to count them on their own. There were two and a quarter million men in the Union army. The only way to verify that there were, or were not, men from the twenty-one western counties of North Carolina assigned to those regiments would be to review the individual service records of all the Union soldiers. I'm confident that a day will come when a computer program will eventually accomplish that.

At the present time, this work seems to be the only modern attempt to count the Union soldiers from western North Carolina. I would urge the reader to consider that I have not reviewed all the Union records. What I have done is search all the reasonable sources for western North Carolina Union soldiers. I have counted all those that I could document and a roster of my count, sorted by county, is contained herein. I have documented the names of 1,636 men that were either born in or said to have resided in one of the twenty-one western North Carolina counties. That count is a far cry from Jones's claim of 4,342.

The reader is advised that I have not counted them all. The question is how many failed to appear in my count. I estimate that the number of men missed in my count would be no more than two hundred. Accordingly, my estimate for Union troops from western North Carolina is 1,836. This estimate would indicate that Jones's count was inflated by approximately twenty-five hundred. Inquiries have failed to identify a source as to where the names of these soldiers might be found.

The other question that emerges when one considers the accuracy of Jones's count is: how did he do it? My primary sources are: the individual service records of the 1st N.C. Infantry; 2nd N.C. Infantry; 2nd N.C. Mounted Infantry; 3rd N.C. Mounted Infantry; the 8th, 9th, and 13th Tennessee Cavalry; the 1st through the 6th U.S. Volunteer Infantry and other Tennessee Infantry regiments; and *North Carolina Troops, 1861-1865*.

It is unlikely that Jones had access to individual records in 1866 and *North Carolina Troops, 1861-1865* wouldn't be available for another century. Jones may have gotten the number from someone in the Union army, or maybe he did some kind of calculation on his own. The problem is that we don't really know where he got the information. Jones offers no sources for his book. He uses the words, "by actual calculation," but he doesn't say whose calculation.

I am not convinced that Jones could have obtained an accurate count of these men in 1866. It just seems unreasonable to me. I raised that question with historians at the U.S. Army Military Institute, and discovered that there is some measure of disagreement on this question. Some historians believe in the possibility that North Carolina's reconstruction Governor Holden, who was an early Unionist, might have been able to obtain that information from someone in the U.S. army. Governor Holden could have acted on Jones's behalf. Perhaps Jones had a direct postwar contact with some source inside the U.S. government. Since Jones never revealed his source it is unlikely that anyone can prove or disprove that Jones or his contacts actually counted western North Carolina men in the Union army at the time. Even in that day one would still be required to examine thousands of individual records in order to get it right.

My main reason for lack of confidence in Jones's count is that I know how difficult such an exercise is today, even with all the new resources available. This difficulty is the likely reason that so many historians have accepted Jones's numbers. It was far easier to accept his count than it was to count them. From a contemporary standpoint one could argue that the "Unionist" position is also a more "politically correct" option.

It is perhaps more likely that Jones was given a count for the men who were in North Carolina Union regiments. That would include North Carolinians from outside western North Carolina as well as men from other states. Several of these regiments were formed on the coast of North Carolina and did not contain any mountain men among their ranks. If Jones or his sources counted the men in those regiments it would have led to a grossly inaccurate count.

There are other claims in Jones's biography that lead to credibility questions. Jones begins his book by pointing out that the vast majority of western North Carolina folks were for the Union prior to Fort Sumter and Lincoln's call for troops to invade the South. This fact is well documented by the election results. In early 1861 western North Carolina voters overwhelmingly voted to stay in the Union. But after Fort Sumter and Lincoln's call to invade the South, everything changed. "My opponent was the same that had run on the Union ticket at the previous election, and was elected by an overwhelming majority over the secession candidate; but he too had gone over to the rebels, and carried all of his friends who had not the moral courage to stick to the Union."[2] In this passage Jones's statements seem to conflict with his later claims of vast Unionism among the populace.

On pages seven, eight, nine, and ten of his book, Jones makes the charge that South Carolina was actually engaged in a clandestine attempt to return the south to British rule. "It is well known to all Americans that in the struggle of our fathers for independence, that there were Tories; men who were opposed to American independence; many perhaps, were honest in regard to their preference for the king and the rule of the mother country. South Carolina by far held more of these Tories than any other State…In 1832 she attempted to nullify the Constitution."[3] Jones might have been the only person who believed that there was any plan to return the colonies to British rule.

Page sixteen contains a strange admission by Jones. "The details and militia were hunting them down [conscripts], though the great body of the militia were Union men, and often aided the party…"[4] Once again there is conflict in Jones's writing. He seems to declare that a vast majority are Union men but on other pages he complains that they are not, or that they are not acting accordingly.

He describes leaving home in August of 1863.[5] He connects with Union sympathizers in Cocke County, Tennessee. He offers little explanation as to where he'd been or what he'd done for nearly two and one-half years of war. Other than saying he had to be quiet and careful he apparently did little toward supporting the Union cause. One might wonder why he didn't go over to the Federal army sooner.

Perhaps the strangest of Jones's claims is that the Confederates were somehow responsible for his daughter's insanity. "An officer entered her [Jones's wife's] chamber, accompanied by her, with the order, in the presence of three grown daughters, the eldest of whom was insane, and now an inmate of the lunatic asylum, caused, as I shall always believe, by the effects of the hated rebellion."[6]

Jones also includes various accounts of suffering and heroic deeds on his part. He is chased, imprisoned, and shot at on numerous occasions, but never hit. He says that it was his role to raise a regiment of North Carolina mountain men. He claims such plans were interrupted by his capture. Apparently the regiment in question was later organized by George W. Kirk and designated the 3rd North Carolina Mounted Infantry (Union).

At the end of his book Jones reveals his political interest when he attacks his likely future competition. As a candidate for Congress he recognized that stiff political opposition was lurking in the form of ex-Confederates. "...But for those who have been leading the rebellion, occupying high positions, military and civil, with all the vindictiveness and ingenuity that could be brought to bear to break up the Union for four years, now to come in and occupy the most responsible positions in the Government, is unreasonable and ought not to be expected; especially those who plied their vocations to this end while holding offices in the Government of the United States previous to the war."[7]

He makes several references to the will of the people being of paramount importance. Apparently he does not wish to adhere to the will of the people if their choice happens to be an ex-Confederate. He may have been sincere in his belief that ex-Confederates should be disqualified on moral grounds but such exclusion was also a crucial part of his political plans and ambitions. He knew they would be tough to beat.

As a parting act, "lame duck" President Andrew Johnson issued at Christmas, 1868, a blanket pardon for all crimes committed during the war. As a result, ex-Confederates were again eligible to vote and hold public office. The Union army no longer controlled the elections and Jones was defeated in 1870.

Throughout his biography Jones implies that he was the rightful leader of the people. He repeatedly espoused his love of his mountain home, yet he chose to live in Washington, D.C., or Maryland after his defeat in 1870. He returned to Asheville for a brief period in the late 1880s. He moved to Oklahoma in 1890, then to California in 1897. Jones died in Long Beach, California, on January 29, 1901.

After all the bombast of his 1866 campaign autobiography one wonders why he never really came home. Jones is little known except to historians and a handful of others who have some special interest in his story. There are no monuments to his service, nor any significant or identifiable public recognition of what he claimed to be. In contrast, the mountain counties are dotted with monuments dedicated to Confederate leaders. When Jones refers to "those leading the rebellion" he seems to be referring to Zeb Vance, the last U.S. Congressman before Jones. While there is no public monument to Jones, there is a monument dedicated to Vance, the epitome of a Confederate leader. The huge stone spire dominates the town square in Asheville, North Carolina. A statue of Vance also rests in Statuary Hall in the U.S. Capitol in Washington, D.C., while Jones seems lost to history.

Jones was a wise, crafty politician dealing with the most difficult time that mountain people had ever faced. He recognized and accepted what others could not or would not recognize. The South had lost the war and the Confederate experience was a disaster. The southern economy was a wreck and mountain people were facing starvation. Jones probably thought, and correctly so, that the best place to get help was from the Union army and the Union government. They had all the money and all the power. Jones was probably sincere in wanting to help his people and felt that the best way to do so was to impress the Union officers.

Probably the most powerful message for Jones at the time of his campaign would have been built around the undeniable fact that the Confederate experience had failed.

It is likely that Jones routinely raised this issue with any receptive audience. He could legitimately point to the maiming, mutilation, and death of our men as well as indescribable suffering on the home front. All the grand promises of Confederate leaders had not only failed but brought with them unbearable suffering. When the shooting stopped and the smoke had cleared mountain families could count nearly six thousand Confederate dead and thousands more wounded in body and mind. The bold southern experiment had ended in disaster and there was no one who could legitimately refute Jones on that critical point.

His claims about Unionism were greatly exaggerated but it didn't matter. He probably felt that if he could convince Union officials that western North Carolina was really Unionist, he would gain favor with them and win the election. He probably had no idea that his exaggerations would be picked up a century later and presented as fact by many historians. Jones exploited what Unionism there was and embellished it to the advantage of himself and his constituents.

His plan to get elected worked as long as the Union army was in full control of western North Carolina. This political environment lasted until the election of 1870 when ex-Confederates swept the state.

REFERENCES
1. Jones, A. H., *Knocking at the Door*, McGill & Witherow, Printers and Stereotypers, Washington, D.C., 1866, page 35.
2. Ibid., page 4.
3. Ibid., pages 7-10.
4. Ibid., page 16.
5. Ibid., page 17.
6. Ibid., page 22.
7. Ibid., page. 37.

TRUE UNIONIST?
James M. Payne and Melinda Reeves Payne with eldest son Robert. Payne resided in Madison County but never joined and was never conscripted into the Confederate army. He crossed the lines in late 1862 and joined the Union army. He was enlisted into the Third North Carolina Mounted Infantry on September 12, 1864. He died of disease in Boone, North Carolina, in March of 1865 while still in Union service.

Chapter Three

──── UNION TROOPS FROM WESTERN NORTH CAROLINA ────
TOTAL ESTIMATE: 1,836

The roster that follows seems to be the first attempt to count western North Carolina men in the Union army since Alexander Hamilton Jones claimed that someone did it in 1866. The difficulty lies in the vast number of men in Union service. Until every record is checked there will always be those who claim that there are others unaccounted for. Even then there is no absolute assurance that the record is correct. Mistakes were made and sometimes the record can mislead the reader.

The methodology of this work involves searching those records that are known to contain the names of such men. It is reasonable to believe that these men were generally attracted to regiments already harboring friends or relatives within their ranks. Of the 1,636 men documented over 70 percent are found in the 2nd and 3rd North Carolina Mounted Infantry Regiment (Union). There were 540 local men in the 2nd NCMI and 632 in the 3rd NCMI. The third largest concentration of local men can be found in the records of the 13th Tennessee Cavalry. The individual service records of that regiment list 160 who were born in, or resided in, a western North Carolina county. There were 161 in the "Galvanized Regiments" and the remaining 142 men are found in the records of various Union units, including the U.S. Navy and Marine Corps as well as units from several northern states identified in *North Carolina Troops, 1861-1865*.

The individual records published in *North Carolina Troops, 1861-1865* lists a small number of former Confederates who "may have served" in the Union army. Since the research included only documented cases these names are not included on my roster.

The reader may choose to disqualify some of the Union men listed for several legitimate reasons. The first possible disqualification is that some of the men on this roster were residents of east Tennessee by the time the war broke out. Some of these men may have been born in western North Carolina but had become long-time residents of another state. It is very difficult to determine how many there might be in that category.

The reverse is also true. There may be some men who don't make this list because their Individual Service Record does not reveal that they had moved to a western North Carolina county. An example is Henry Correll, who joined the Union army in late 1863. He is not included on the roster that follows because there is nothing in his record that indicates he was from a western North Carolina county. The record indicates that he was born in Rowan County, but he may have later moved to Madison County. The family believes that he may have moved here prior to the war but there is no such documentation in his service record.

The service records contain at least four possible places for such information: the original enlistment record, the company descriptive book or roll, medical or hospital records, and death certificates. In most cases the only identifying information regarding a soldier's home county is the company descriptive book. On that page of the individual record the recording officer simply filled in a blank labeled, "Where born." The same is true of the original enlistment record. In the case of hospital or death records the documents may indicate where the soldier resided at the time.

Another possible disqualification is related to those who may have considered themselves forced to join the Union army. Approximately 293 men are documented to have joined in order to escape possible death or torture in a Union prison camp.[1] No attempt to exclude them was used in preparing this work. While some men may have had genuine Unionist convictions, survival was probably a more significant motivation.

The Confederates who joined at Union prisons and others were sometimes called "Galvanized Yankees." Six regiments were formed for the purpose of recruiting Confederates with the promise of being sent out west to serve on the frontier. These units were the 1st through the 6th U.S. Volunteer Infantry Regiments. A total of 161 western North Carolina men joined these units and headed west. A review of the compiled service records was done in order to determine if desertion rates among these men were consistent with the claims of Hezekiah Thomas.[1] The numbers are as follows for each of the six regiments:

Regt.	WNC men	killed	wounds	War time desertions	Postwar desertions	Total desertions
1st U.S.	81	0	0	4	9	13
2nd U.S.	5	0	0	0	0	0
3rd U.S.	11	0	0	0	0	0
4th U.S.	9	0	0	0	3	3
5th U.S.	21	0	0	0	11	11
6th U.S.	34	0	0	0	18	18
TOTAL	161	0	0	4	41	45 (28%)

Approximately 10 percent of the records for these men could not be located under the spelling found in *North Carolina Troops, 1861-1865*. Some historians would rate a war-time desertion as more significant than a postwar desertion. It has been recognized that at war's end some Union veterans, from a wide variety of units, felt that they had completed their service. They did not enlist as an occupying force; for them the war was over. Therefore, many just packed up and went home.

A postwar desertion might also indicate that the men were anti-Confederates using the Union army as a place to avoid Confederate conscription and combat. Joining one of the "Galvanized Regiments" offered many advantages. One could escape Union prisons and the war with a trip out west. The records indicate that these men worked as cooks, sutlers, blacksmiths, loggers, and wagon train guards.[2] They received pay and ate regularly, something that would not have occurred if they had remained in the Confederate army or in a Union prison. It may have been tough duty at times, but as it turned out there was little chance of being killed or wounded.

One should recognize that these "Galvanized" soldiers could not foretell the future. They would not have known for sure what fate awaited them on the western frontier, but they were very certain of what was happening on the battlefields of the east. If they had remained with the Army of Northern Virginia there was a high probability of being killed or mutilated. If they remained in a Union prison there was about a 20 to 25 percent chance they would have died.

The train ride out west must have been a strange experience for these mountaineers. Their minds must have been spinning with thoughts of home, the war, and the men they had left behind in prison. They were heading into the unknown; as frightening as that may have been, it was probably a very attractive option. They may not have known where they were going, but they knew they had left hell behind.

REFERENCES
1. Jordan, Weymouth T., and Louis H. Manarin, *North Carolina Troops, 1861-1865: A Roster*, North Carolina Office of Archives and History, Department of Cultural Resources, 1966.
2. National Archives of the United States, Compiled Service Records of the First through the Sixth U.S. Volunteer Infantry, Record Group No. 94, Microfilm No. 1017, 1978.

THOMAS, HEZEKIAH, Private

Born in Watauga County* in 1846. Was by occupation a farmer prior to enlisting in Watauga County on July 18, 1862, for the war. Reported present in January-June, 1863. Reported sick in hospital in September-October, 1863. Returned to duty in November-December, 1863. Reported present through August 31, 1864. Captured at Jonesborough, Georgia, September 5, 1864. Sent to Nashville, Tennessee. Transferred to Louisville, Kentucky, where he arrived on October 28, 1864. Transferred to Camp Douglas, Chicago, Illinois, where he arrived on November 1, 1864. Released at Camp Douglas on May 5, 1865, after joining the U.S. Army. Assigned to Company C, 6th Regiment U.S. Volunteer Infantry. [His Tennessee pension application states that he and "thousands more" enlisted in the Federal army at Camp Douglas because "we were all about to starve to death." After he enlisted in the Federal army he was "taken out to Fort Kerney, in Nebraska(,) and from there I was taken to Grand Island (Nebraska) to make hay for the Government and while there some of the Government horses was stolen and ... (I was detailed with a corporal) to go ... hunt for the horses; so we followed the horses for about 400 miles, and after we got there we decided to come home and we never went back to get our discharge."]

Copying and republication authorized by the North Carolina Office of Archives and History from North Carolina Troops, 1861-1865: A Roster, Volume 15, Company D, 58th North Carolina Infantry Regiment

UNION SERVICE ROSTER
WESTERN NORTH CAROLINA
1861-1865

County	Men in Service
Ashe	70
Buncombe	389
Burke	28
Caldwell	51
Catawba	10
Cherokee	46
Clay	7
Cleveland	12
Haywood	31
Henderson	130
Jackson	27
Macon	22
Madison	135
McDowell	44
Mitchell	84
Polk	12
Rutherford	52
Transylvania	13
Watauga	47
Wilkes	145
Yancey	281
Estimated Omissions	200
Total Men in Service	1,836

ASHE COUNTY UNION SOLDIERS

	Name	Regiment	Company	Date of Enlistment
1	Anderson, Riley	13th TN Cav.	D	09/24/1863
2	Baker, James M.	1st US Vol. Inft.	E	02/18/1864
3	Bare, Jessie	?	?	01/24/1864
4	Billings, William	3rd NC Mtd. Inft.	B	07/18/1864
5	Blackburn, Thomas	3rd NC Mtd. Inft.	F	03/11/1865
6	Bumgardner, David	13th TN Cav.	I	01/14/1864
7	Burgess, Thomas	?	?	01/26/1864
8	Cornutt, David E.	13th TN Cav.	G	10/25/1863
9	Cornutt, Isaac	13th TN Cav.	G	01/15/1864
10	Cornutt, Wiley	13th TN Cav.	G	10/25/1863
11	Daugherty, John H.	13th TN Cav.	D	09/23/1863
12	Davis, William	1st US Vol. Inft.	B	02/02/1864
13	Eggers, John	13th TN Cav.	I	01/13/1864
14	Eller, Jacob	13th TN Cav.	D	10/01/1864
15	Elliott, Stephen	3rd US Vol. Inft.	H	10/31/1864
16	Esteridge, Barnabas	6th US Vol. Inft.	G	03/14/1865
17	Esteridge, John	1st US Vol. Inft.	C	01/25/1864
18	Esteridge, William	13th TN Cav.	E	10/01/1864
19	Farington, Hugh	1st US Vol. Inft.	C	01/26/1864
20	Flannery, Joseph	13th TN Cav.	E	10/28/1863
21	Gibbs, Franklin	13th TN Cav.	C	01/20/1864
22	Gilly, George C.	13th TN Cav.	D	10/28/1863
23	Goss, William	1st US Vol. Inft.	I	02/02/1864
24	Graybeal, David	13th TN Cav.	E	10/01/1864
25	Graybeal, Reuben	13th TN Cav.	E	09/24/1863
26	Graybeal, William	13th TN Cav.	E	09/24/1863
27	Grear, Hamilton	13th TN Cav.	E	09/22/1863
28	Greene, Allen	2nd NC Mtd. Inft.	E	04/15/1865
29	Greenweld, John	13th TN Cav.	I	09/22/1863

30	Greer, Andrew	13th TN Cav.	I	09/22/1863
31	Greer, John	13th TN Cav.	I	05/31/1864
32	Hilliard, James R.	13th TN Cav.	I	07/01/1864
33	Hilton, John W.	US Navy		02/05/1864
34	Howell, Alvin P.	?	?	10/06/1864
35	Kilby, William	13th TN Cav.	I	01/15/1864
36	King, James	13th TN Cav.	D	10/28/1863
37	Lewis, Alexander	13th TN Cav.	I	01/15/1864
38	Lewis, James	13th TN Cav.	I	01/15/1864
39	McCoy, Hiram	13th TN Cav.	E	10/01/1864
40	Merrill, A. B.	US Navy		12/09/1863
41	Michael, Creed	3rd NC Mtd. Inft.	I	03/08/1865
42	Michael, Frederick	3rd NC Mtd. Inft.	A	06/11/1864
43	Michael, Lorenzo D.	3rd NC Mtd. Inft.	F	07/01/1864
44	Miller, James L.	13th TN Cav.	I	01/15/1864
45	Newton, Alvin	3rd NC Mtd. Inft.	B	06/01/1864
46	Nuves, Henry	3rd NC Mtd. Inft.	A	06/11/1864
47	Osborn, Aris	13th TN Cav.	G	09/24/1863
48	Osborn, Jeremiah	13th TN Cav.	E	09/21/1863
49	Osborne, David	3rd NC Mtd. Inft.	D	03/03/1864
50	Pennington, William	4th US Vol. Inft.	C	10/17/1864
51	Phillips, Columbus	3rd NC Mtd. Inft.	F	11/11/1864
52	Phillips, William	3rd NC Mtd. Inft.	H	01/25/1865
53	Roalten, William	13th TN Cav.	I	10/15/1864
54	Roark, Alfred W.	3rd NC Mtd. Inft.	B	06/23/1864
55	Roark, Ephram	13th TN Cav.	G	10/28/1863
56	Robbins, James	3rd NC Mtd. Inft.	I	03/08/1865
57	Roller, Reuben	13th TN Cav.	I	01/15/1864
58	Rose, Wyatt	US Navy		?
59	Rotan, Jacob	13th TN Cav.	G	09/24/1863
60	Sanders, Alexander	1st US Vol. Inft.	A	01/22/1864

61	Sluder, Felix	US Navy		01/25/1864
62	South, George	13th TN Cav.	F	09/01/1864
63	Story, Noah	13th TN Cav.	E	09/24/1863
64	Taylor, Eli	13th TN Cav.	G	09/01/1865
65	Tomlinson, Hiram	1st US Vol. Inft.	I	05/27/1864
66	Vanover, Ripley	13th TN Cav.	G	10/28/1863
67	Walker, Ishan	3rd NC Mtd. Inft.	G	10/01/1864
68	White, Leander	3rd NC Mtd. Inft.	B	07/17/1864
69	Williams, Thomas	13th TN Cav.	E	09/24/1863
70	Younce, Elijah	13th TN Cav.	G	11/01/1864

BUNCOMBE COUNTY UNION SOLDIERS

	Name	Regiment	Company	Date of Enlistment
1	Alexander, James E.	5th US Vol. Inft.	I	04/15/1865
2	Allen, William	3rd NC Mtd. Inft.	J	03/01/1865
3	Anders, Hiram	3rd NC Mtd. Inft.	K	03/01/1865
4	Anders, John C.	2nd NC Mtd. Inft.	B	10/01/1863
5	Anderson, Robert	2nd NC Mtd. Inft.	C	09/26/1863
6	Anderson, William	2nd NC Mtd. Inft.	C	09/26/1863
7	Anderson, William W.	2nd NC Mtd. Inft.	F	10/01/1863
8	Arrowood, Hughey G.	3rd NC Mtd. Inft.	C	04/04/1864
9	Arrowood, Edmund	2nd NC Mtd. Inft.	B	10/01/1863
10	Arrowood, James P.	2nd NC Mtd. Inft.	B	09/25/1863
11	Arwood, Robert D.	3rd NC Mtd. Inft.	H	01/25/1865
12	Ball, Jeremiah C.	2nd NC Mtd. Inft.	B	05/01/1864
13	Ball, Manly	2nd NC Mtd. Inft.	C	10/01/1863
14	Ballard, James R.	3rd NC Mtd. Inft.	G	01/15/1865
15	Ballenger, James	2nd NC Mtd. Inft.	B	10/06/1863
16	Barnett, Levi W.	2nd NC Mtd. Inft.	A	09/15/1863
17	Barnett, Zachariah	2nd NC Mtd. Inft.	A	09/15/1863
18	Barrett, Jesse R.	3rd NC Mtd. Inft.	?	04/20/1864
19	Barrett, Christopher	2nd NC Mtd. Inft.	B	09/25/1863
20	Barrett, David	2nd NC Mtd. Inft.	D	10/01/1863
21	Barrett, Jesse R.	2nd NC Mtd. Inft.	B	05/01/1864
22	Barrett, John E.	2nd NC Mtd. Inft.	B	09/25/1863
23	Beachboard, Alexander	2nd NC Mtd. Inft.	B	09/25/1863
24	Beachboard, Lorenzo D.	2nd NC Mtd. Inft.	B	09/25/1863
25	Beavers, James W.	2nd NC Mtd. Inft.	C	09/26/1863
26	Black, Jesse L.	3rd NC Mtd. Inft.	G	01/01/1865
27	Blythe, George F.	2nd NC Mtd. Inft.	F	10/01/1863
28	Blythe, Gilford I.	2nd NC Mtd. Inft.	F	10/01/1863

29	Blythe, Robert O.	2nd NC Mtd. Inft.	F	10/01/1863
30	Brackens, James	2nd NC Mtd. Inft.	F	06/01/1864
31	Bradburn, Bluford	2nd NC Mtd. Inft.	C	05/01/1864
32	Bradburn, David F.	2nd NC Mtd. Inft.	C	12/30/1864
33	Brank, David V.	2nd NC Mtd. Inft.	B	10/06/1863
34	Brank, J. Washington	2nd NC Mtd. Inft.	B	10/06/1863
35	Brank, Mitchell A.	2nd NC Mtd. Inft.	B	10/25/1863
36	Brank, Winfield	2nd NC Mtd. Inft.	B	10/25/1863
37	Briggs, Garrett	2nd NC Mtd. Inft.	A	10/25/1863
38	Briggs, George W.	2nd NC Mtd. Inft.	A	10/25/1863
39	Briggs, John G.	2nd NC Mtd. Inft.	A	10/25/1863
40	Briggs, Wilson	2nd NC Mtd. Inft.	A	10/25/1863
41	Briton, Joseph	3rd NC Mtd. Inft.	B	06/18/1864
42	Brooks, James	3rd NC Mtd. Inft.	C	09/12/1864
43	Brown, Adolphus E.	US Navy		06/10/1864
44	Brown, John	2nd NC Mtd. Inft.	B	01/15/1865
45	Bryan, George W.	2nd NC Mtd. Inft.	A	05/01/1864
46	Bryan, Lewis (Levi)	2nd NC Mtd. Inft.	A	09/15/1863
47	Buckner, Alfred M.	2nd NC Mtd. Inft.	A	09/15/1863
48	Buckner, David	2nd NC Mtd. Inft.	F	10/01/1863
49	Buckner, George	2nd NC Mtd. Inft.	A	09/15/1863
50	Buckner, Harrison H.	2nd NC Mtd. Inft.	A	10/01/1864
51	Buckner, Harvey P.	3rd NC Mtd. Inft.	K	03/01/1865
52	Buckner, James M.	2nd NC Mtd. Inft.	A	09/15/1863
53	Buckner, Jeremiah	2nd NC Mtd. Inft.	B	09/15/1863
54	Buckner, John H.	2nd NC Mtd. Inft.	A	09/15/1863
55	Buckner, Nimrod	2nd NC Mtd. Inft.	A	09/15/1863
56	Buckner, Noah	3rd NC Mtd. Inft.	C	03/01/1865
57	Buckner, Squire	2nd NC Mtd. Inft.	F	10/01/1863
58	Buckner, Stephen M.	3rd NC Mtd. Inft.	K	03/01/1865
59	Buckner, Philip	2nd NC Mtd. Inft.	A	04/01/1864

60	Burleson, Daniel W.	2nd NC Mtd. Inft.	H	05/04/1864
61	Burleson, Samuel M.	3rd NC Mtd. Inft.	G	02/12/1865
62	Burnett, Edward	2nd NC Mtd. Inft.	F	10/01/1863
63	Caldwell, Henry E.	2nd NC Mtd. Inft.	C	10/01/1863
64	Candler, James	2nd NC Mtd. Inft.	E	09/01/1863
65	Cantrell, John	2nd NC Mtd. Inft.	F	10/01/1863
66	Cantrell, Levi	2nd NC Mtd. Inft.	F	10/01/1863
67	Capps, John D.	US Navy		06/10/1864
68	Carland, Franklin B.	2nd NC Mtd. Inft.	H	01/16/1865
69	Carter, Abraham	3rd NC Mtd. Inft.	G	03/25/1864
70	Carter, John H.	3rd NC Mtd. Inft.	K	03/01/1865
71	Carter, William	2nd NC Mtd. Inft.	B	09/25/1863
72	Carter, William	3rd NC Mtd. Inft.	H	10/01/1864
73	Carter, William H.	3rd NC Mtd. Inft.	K	03/01/1865
74	Carter, Wilson	2nd NC Mtd. Inft.	A	09/15/1863
75	Case, Andrew	2nd NC Mtd. Inft.	F	10/01/1863
76	Case, Elijah F.	2nd NC Mtd. Inft.	F	10/01/1863
77	Case, James M.	2nd NC Mtd. Inft.	F	10/01/1863
78	Case, Joshua F.	2nd NC Mtd. Inft.	F	10/01/1863
79	Case, William	2nd NC Mtd. Inft.	F	10/01/1863
80	Chambers, Joseph B.	3rd NC Mtd. Inft.	K	03/01/1865
81	Chambers, William K.	3rd NC Mtd. Inft.	K	03/09/1865
82	Citton, Kinsey	3rd NC Mtd. Inft.	I	01/01/1865
83	Clark, Jacob	2nd NC Mtd. Inft.	B	10/01/1863
84	Clark, James E.	2nd NC Mtd. Inft.	B	09/25/1863
85	Clark, Samuel	2nd NC Mtd. Inft.	F	10/01/1863
86	Clemens, James	2nd NC Mtd. Inft.	A	09/15/1863
87	Club, William	2nd NC Mtd. Inft.	A	09/15/1863
88	Coates, Garrett	3rd NC Mtd. Inft.	G	01/12/1865
89	Coggins, Henry A.	6th US Vol. Inft.	D	12/22/1864
90	Cole, Francis Marion	3rd US Vol. Inft.	D	10/15/1864

91	Cole, James H.	2nd NC Mtd. Inft.	B	09/25/1863
92	Cole, Thomas D.	2nd NC Mtd. Inft.	D	09/25/1863
93	Cole, William H.	5th US Vol. Inft.	F	04/06/1865
94	Combs, Jefferson	3rd NC Mtd. Inft.	C	06/11/1864
95	Cordell, Adolphus	3rd NC Mtd. Inft.	G	02/16/1865
96	Cordell, Daniel	3rd NC Mtd. Inft.	G	02/16/1865
97	Cordell, Soloman	5th US Vol. Inft.	F	04/06/1865
98	Corn, Hughes B.	3rd NC Mtd. Inft.	E	03/01/1865
99	Crowder, Elijah B.	2nd NC Mtd. Inft.	A	09/15/1863
100	Crowder, Elsberry	2nd NC Mtd. Inft.	A	09/15/1863
101	Crowder, James A.	2nd NC Mtd. Inft.	A	10/01/1863
102	Curtis, Thomas	3rd US Vol. Inft.	F	10/17/1864
103	Davis, Alfred N.	2nd NC Mtd. Inft.	A	09/15/1863
104	Davis, David F.	2nd NC Mtd. Inft.	C	03/01/1864
105	Davis, George W.	2nd NC Mtd. Inft.	D	10/03/1863
106	Davis, Jackson	3rd NC Mtd. Inft.	C	03/25/1864
107	Davis, James M.	2nd NC Mtd. Inft.	B	10/07/1863
108	Davis, John	2nd NC Mtd. Inft.	C	03/01/1864
109	Davis, John E.	2nd NC Mtd. Inft.	C	10/01/1863
110	Davis, Minsey	2nd NC Mtd. Inft.	C	09/26/1863
111	Davis, Peter	2nd NC Mtd. Inft.	C	09/26/1863
112	Deaver, William H.	2nd NC Mtd. Inft.	B	05/01/1864
113	Devers, Shepard	2nd NC Mtd. Inft.	B	05/01/1864
114	Dockery, Elijah	2nd NC Mtd. Inft.	C	10/01/1864
115	Done, Morgan	3rd NC Mtd. Inft.	K	03/01/1865
116	Done, Zachariah T.	3rd NC Mtd. Inft.	K	03/01/1865
117	Dover, William	3rd NC Mtd. Inft.	C	10/08/1864
118	Dryman, James	3rd NC Mtd. Inft.	F	09/20/1864
119	Dula, Elbert Sidney	3rd US Vol. Inft.	F	10/17/1864
120	Edmonds, John G.	2nd NC Mtd. Inft.	B	10/03/1863
121	Edwards, Allen	3rd NC Mtd. Inft.	I	03/01/1865

122	Edwards, Timothy	3rd NC Mtd. Inft.	I	03/01/1865
123	Eller, Adam B.	2nd NC Mtd. Inft.	B	09/25/1863
124	Eller, Adam F.	2nd NC Mtd. Inft.	B	09/25/1863
125	Eller, John W.	3rd NC Mtd. Inft.	B	07/03/1864
126	Eller, Thomas	3rd NC Mtd. Inft.	B	07/03/1864
127	Eller, William E.	2nd NC Mtd. Inft.	B	01/01/1865
128	Ensley, John	3rd NC Mtd. Inft.	H	01/25/1865
129	Evans, Henry P.	2nd NC Mtd. Inft.	F	10/01/1863
130	Feagan, William J.	13th TN Cav.	M	05/15/1864
131	Fisher, Jesse	2nd NC Mtd. Inft.	A	09/15/1863
132	Fisher, William	3rd NC Mtd. Inft.	C	11/05/1864
133	Foster, Robert	2nd NC Mtd. Inft.	A	04/01/1864
134	Fox, Alfred	2nd NC Mtd. Inft.	A	09/15/1863
135	Fox, Alfred M.	2nd NC Mtd. Inft.	A	09/15/1863
136	Fox, Allen	2nd NC Mtd. Inft.	A	09/15/1863
137	Fox, Elbert	2nd NC Mtd. Inft.	A	09/15/1863
138	Fox, James M.	2nd NC Mtd. Inft.	A	09/15/1863
139	Fox, John	2nd NC Mtd. Inft.	A	09/15/1863
140	Fox, John N.	2nd NC Mtd. Inft.	A	04/01/1864
141	Fox, Lafayette	2nd NC Mtd. Inft.	B	09/25/1863
142	Fox, Melvin	3rd NC Mtd. Inft.	G	02/01/1865
143	Fox, Pinkney	2nd NC Mtd. Inft.	B	09/25/1863
144	Fox, Robert L.	2nd NC Mtd. Inft.	B	09/25/1863
145	Franks, Henry	2nd NC Mtd. Inft.	D	06/15/1864
146	Franks, Henry	3rd NC Mtd. Inft.	C	07/26/1864
147	Franks, Joshua	2nd NC Mtd. Inft.	D	10/03/1863
148	Freeman, Andrew J.	2nd NC Mtd. Inft.	C	09/26/1863
149	Freeman, Benjamin F.	2nd NC Mtd. Inft.	C	10/01/1864
150	Freeman, Daniel E.	2nd NC Mtd. Inft.	C	09/26/1863
151	Freeman, George W.	2nd NC Mtd. Inft.	C	09/26/1863
152	Freeman, Seth	2nd NC Mtd. Inft.	C	09/26/1863

153	Frisby, Lorenzo	2nd NC Mtd. Inft.	B	01/15/1865
154	Gentry, Lewis	3rd NC Mtd. Inft.	K	03/01/1865
155	Gentry, Perimeter M.	3rd NC Mtd. Inft.	C	07/02/1864
156	Gentry, Thomas J.	2nd NC Mtd. Inft.	B	05/01/1864
157	Gillespie, John	2nd NC Mtd. Inft.	A	09/15/1863
158	Gillespie, Phillip	2nd NC Mtd. Inft.	F	10/01/1863
159	Gillespie, Wilson	2nd NC Mtd. Inft.	B	10/01/1864
160	Glazener, Albert	2nd NC Mtd. Inft.	F	06/01/1864
161	Gragg, John S.	1st US Vol. Inft.	D	05/01/1864
162	Graham, Columbus	3rd NC Mtd. Inft.	A	11/01/1864
163	Griggs, James P.	5th US Vol. Inft.	F	04/06/1865
164	Grooms, James	2nd NC Mtd. Inft.	A	04/01/1864
165	Guthrie, John W.	3rd NC Mtd. Inft.	K	03/01/1865
166	Guthrie, Thaddeus O.	3rd NC Mtd. Inft.	K	03/01/1865
167	Guthrie, William H.	2nd NC Mtd. Inft.	A	09/15/1863
168	Hagans, Colston G.	2nd NC Mtd. Inft.	C	09/26/1863
169	Hall, George W.	2nd US Vol. Inft.	I	10/13/1864
170	Hamblen (Hamlin), William	2nd NC Mtd. Inft.	F	12/14/1863
171	Hamilton, Hughey C.	2nd NC Mtd. Inft.	B	10/01/1863
172	Hamilton, Joseph	2nd NC Mtd. Inft.	F	09/26/1863
173	Hamilton, Robert F.	2nd NC Mtd. Inft.	B	10/01/1863
174	Hamilton, Voltaire	2nd NC Mtd. Inft.	F	10/01/1863
175	Hamilton, William H.	2nd NC Mtd. Inft.	B	10/01/1863
176	Hampton, John	3rd NC Mtd. Inft.	B	06/23/1864
177	Hampton, Turley	3rd NC Mtd. Inft.	B	06/20/1864
178	Haren, Archibald L.	3rd US Vol. Inft.	F	10/17/1864
179	Haren, Judson D.	2nd NC Mtd. Inft.	B	10/01/1863
180	Harland, James	2nd NC Mtd. Inft.	E	09/01/1863
181	Harris, John A.	2nd NC Mtd. Inft.	B	09/25/1863
182	Heatherly, Moses	2nd NC Mtd. Inft.	H	05/06/1864
183	Hembree, Joseph C.	1st US Vol. Inft.	F	02/24/1864

184	Henderson, Charles	2nd NC Mtd. Inft.	B	10/01/1863
185	Henderson, Leonard W.	2nd NC Mtd. Inft.	A	09/15/1863
186	Henderson, Robert B.	2nd NC Mtd. Inft.	A	09/15/1863
187	Hensley, Charles W.	3rd NC Mtd. Inft.	K	03/01/1865
188	Hensley, Elijah	3rd NC Mtd. Inft.	K	03/01/1865
189	Herron, Joshua	3rd NC Mtd. Inft.	C	09/25/1864
190	Hildebrand, Ohio	3rd NC Mtd. Inft.	I	03/06/1865
191	Holcombe, Isaac	3rd NC Mtd. Inft.	C	03/01/1865
192	Hood, James B.	2nd NC Mtd. Inft.	D	10/03/1863
193	Huggins, John B.	2nd NC Mtd. Inft.	F	10/01/1863
194	Huggins, Langford	2nd NC Mtd. Inft.	F	10/01/1863
195	Hughey, Hamilton H.	2nd NC Mtd. Inft.	D	10/03/1863
196	Hughey, James	2nd NC Mtd. Inft.	A	05/01/1864
197	Hughey, Samuel G.	2nd NC Mtd. Inft.	A	09/15/1863
198	Hughey, William	6th US Vol. Inft.	F	03/26/1865
199	Hughey, William	3rd NC Mtd. Inft.	C	10/08/1864
200	Hunter, Andrew J.	2nd NC Mtd. Inft.	A	09/15/1863
201	Hunter, Thomas	2nd NC Mtd. Inft.	A	09/15/1863
202	Hunter, Wiley C.	2nd NC Mtd. Inft.	A	08/01/1864
203	Hunter, William R.	2nd NC Mtd. Inft.	A	09/15/1863
204	Ingle, Eavans	6th US Vol. Inft.	D	05/24/1865
205	Ingle, Robert H.	2nd NC Mtd. Inft.	A	04/01/1864
206	Jenkins, Francis N.	3rd NC Mtd. Inft.	I	03/01/1865
207	Jones, Isaac C.	2nd NC Mtd. Inft.	B	04/15/1865
208	Justus, James N.	2nd NC Mtd. Inft.	B	09/25/1863
209	Keith, Caleb N.	2nd NC Mtd. Inft.	A	04/17/1865
210	Kerley, Richard	3rd NC Mtd. Inft.	I	03/01/1865
211	King, Martin A.	3rd NC Mtd. Inft.	C	12/30/1864
212	Kirkendall, Isaac	2nd NC Mtd. Inft.	B	10/01/1863
213	Kirkendall, Thomas M.	2nd NC Mtd. Inft.	B	10/01/1863
214	Kuykendall, Jahew (John)	2nd NC Mtd. Inft.	H	10/01/1863

215	Lankford, William J.	2nd NC Mtd. Inft.	B	04/01/1864
216	Ledford, Joseph	2nd NC Mtd. Inft.	C	09/26/1863
217	Ledford, Joseph S.	3rd NC Mtd. Inft.	C	09/23/1864
218	Ledford, Obidiah	3rd NC Mtd. Inft.	B	07/02/1864
219	Lewis, Robert	3rd NC Mtd. Inft.	E	09/16/1864
220	Lindsey, Thomas	6th US Vol. Inft.	I	04/02/1865
221	Lockaby, George W.	2nd NC Mtd. Inft.	D	10/11/1863
222	Lunsford, David	2nd NC Mtd. Inft.	C	10/01/1864
223	Lunsford, Eli	2nd NC Mtd. Inft.	C	10/01/1863
224	Lunsford, Ephraim	2nd NC Mtd. Inft.	C	04/01/1865
225	Lunsford, Henry	2nd NC Mtd. Inft.	C	09/26/1863
226	Lunsford, James	2nd NC Mtd. Inft.	C	10/01/1864
227	Lunsford, Jeremiah	2nd NC Mtd. Inft.	C	09/26/1863
228	Lunsford, Levi	2nd NC Mtd. Inft.	C	09/26/1863
229	Mann, William	2nd NC Mtd. Inft.	C	09/26/1863
230	Massey, Andrew J.	2nd NC Mtd. Inft.	A	09/15/1863
231	Massey, Jefferson	2nd NC Mtd. Inft.	B	10/01/1863
232	Massey, Samuel	2nd NC Mtd. Inft.	A	09/15/1863
233	McFalls, Daniel	US Navy		12/26/1863
234	McGaha, Joseph	2nd NC Mtd. Inft.	F	11/07/1864
235	McKinney, John	2nd NC Mtd. Inft.	B	12/05/1864
236	Melton, Lewis E.	3rd NC Mtd. Inft.	E	03/25/1864
237	Miller, John H.	6th US Vol. Inft.	F	03/26/1865
238	Morgan, James N.	3rd NC Mtd. Inft.	K	03/01/1865
239	Munson, Robert S.	2nd NC Mtd. Inft.	A	09/15/1863
240	Munson, Pierce R.	2nd NC Mtd. Inft.	A	10/01/1863
241	Oliver, Resa	2nd NC Mtd. Inft.	A	09/15/1863
242	Orr, Caleb	2nd NC Mtd. Inft.	F	10/01/1863
243	Osteen, Elijah	2nd NC Mtd. Inft.	C	10/01/1863
244	Osteen, Elisha	2nd NC Mtd. Inft.	B	10/01/1863
245	Pack, George W.	2nd US Vol. Inft.	B	10/06/1864

246	Paine, Daniel	2nd NC Mtd. Inft.	C	09/26/1863
247	Paine, Isaiah	2nd NC Mtd. Inft.	C	09/26/1863
248	Paine, James	2nd NC Mtd. Inft.	C	09/26/1863
249	Paine, John H.	2nd NC Mtd. Inft.	B	09/25/1863
250	Palmer, John A.	3rd NC Mtd. Inft.	H	01/25/1865
251	Pane, James	2nd NC Mtd. Inft.	C	10/03/1863
252	Pannel, William T.	6th IN Cav.	G	09/01/1863
253	Panther, John	2nd NC Mtd. Inft.	H	01/23/1864
254	Paris, Jackson	2nd NC Mtd. Inft.	C	09/26/1863
255	Parker, John F.	3rd NC Mtd. Inft.	C	05/11/1864
256	Parker, Thomas M.	3rd NC Mtd. Inft.	C	05/11/1864
257	Patterson, William	3rd NC Mtd. Inft.	C	10/05/1864
258	Patton, Robert	2nd NC Mtd. Inft.	F	10/01/1863
259	Payne, Isaiah	2nd NC Mtd. Inft.	F	10/01/1863
260	Payne, James M.	2nd NC Mtd. Inft.	C	09/26/1863
261	Peek, Garrett	2nd NC Mtd. Inft.	A	09/15/1863
262	Peek, William Henry	2nd NC Mtd. Inft.	A	09/15/1863
263	Pendland, Robert B.	3rd NC Mtd. Inft.	C	03/01/1865
264	Penland, James R.	2nd NC Mtd. Inft.	B	09/25/1863
265	Perry, William D.	2nd NC Mtd. Inft.	C	09/26/1863
266	Pickens, John C.	2nd NC Mtd. Inft.	B	09/25/1863
267	Pickens, Robert H.	2nd NC Mtd. Inft.	B	09/25/1863
268	Powers, John	5th US Vol. Inft.	F	04/06/1865
269	Ramsey, Jackson	2nd NC Mtd. Inft.	C	10/01/1863
270	Ramsey, James	2nd NC Mtd. Inft.	B	10/01/1863
271	Ramsey, Jobe	2nd NC Mtd. Inft.	C	09/26/1863
272	Ramsey, Lewis W.	2nd NC Mtd. Inft.	C	09/26/1863
273	Ramsey, Robert	2nd NC Mtd. Inft.	B	10/01/1863
274	Ramsey, William W.	2nd NC Mtd. Inft.	C	09/26/1863
275	Randall, John B.	2nd NC Mtd. Inft.	C	09/26/1863
276	Rash, Martin	2nd NC Mtd. Inft.	C	05/01/1864

277	Ray, Thomas	2nd NC Mtd. Inft.	C	04/01/1864
278	Rector, Alfred	3rd NC Mtd. Inft.	C	08/20/1864
279	Rector, Enoch	2nd NC Mtd. Inft.	E	01/21/1865
280	Rector, Franklin	3rd NC Mtd. Inft.	C	09/06/1864
281	Rector, Julius	3rd NC Mtd. Inft.	C	09/01/1864
282	Rector, Samuel	2nd NC Mtd. Inft.	C	09/26/1863
283	Reese, Martin V.	2nd NC Mtd. Inft.	B	09/25/1863
284	Reese, Patterson	2nd NC Mtd. Inft.	B	09/25/1863
285	Reese, William R.	2nd NC Mtd. Inft.	B	09/25/1863
286	Revis, Alford Goodson	2nd NC Mtd. Inft.	B	01/15/1865
287	Revis, Henry M.	2nd NC Mtd. Inft.	B	09/25/1863
288	Revis, Jacob M.	2nd NC Mtd. Inft.	B	09/25/1863
289	Revis, Thomas H.	3rd NC Mtd. Inft.	H	01/01/1865
290	Rice, Job	2nd NC Mtd. Inft.	A	09/15/1863
291	Rice, Joseph L.	2nd NC Mtd. Inft.	A	05/01/1864
292	Rice, Spencer	2nd NC Mtd. Inft.	B	10/01/1863
293	Rice, Wesley	3rd NC Mtd. Inft.	G	02/01/1865
294	Roberts, Andrew J.	2nd NC Mtd. Inft.	E	10/01/1863
295	Roberts, George	2nd NC Mtd. Inft.	B	01/10/1865
296	Roberts, George M.	2nd NC Mtd. Inft.	B	04/01/1864
297	Roberts, George W.	2nd NC Mtd. Inft.	C	09/26/1863
298	Roberts, Henry C.	3rd NC Mtd. Inft.	A	06/11/1864
299	Roberts, John	2nd NC Mtd. Inft.	A	09/15/1863
300	Roberts, John J.	3rd NC Mtd. Inft.	A	06/11/1864
301	Roberts, John P.	2nd NC Mtd. Inft.	A	09/15/1863
302	Roberts, Ninevah	2nd NC Mtd. Inft.	A	09/15/1863
303	Roberts, Robert K.	3rd NC Mtd. Inft.	I	03/01/1865
304	Roberts, Stephen	2nd NC Mtd. Inft.	B	10/01/1863
305	Roberts, William R.	3rd NC Mtd. Inft.	A	06/11/1864
306	Roberts, Wyley S.	3rd NC Mtd. Inft.	E	03/01/1865
307	Rogers, Jasper	3rd NC Mtd. Inft.	H	02/16/1865

308	Rogers, Perry	2nd NC Mtd. Inft.	B	09/25/1863
309	Rogers, William	2nd NC Mtd. Inft.	B	09/25/1863
310	Sams, Anson	2nd NC Mtd. Inft.	A	09/15/1863
311	Sams, Zephaniah	2nd NC Mtd. Inft.	A	09/15/1863
312	Sawyer, Archibald	2nd NC Mtd. Inft.	A	09/15/1863
313	Sawyer, Lewis S.	2nd NC Mtd. Inft.	A	10/01/1863
314	Sentell, Guilford	2nd NC Mtd. Inft.	F	10/01/1863
315	Sentell, James L.	2nd NC Mtd. Inft.	F	10/01/1863
316	Sentell, Jesse B.	2nd NC Mtd. Inft.	F	10/01/1863
317	Sentell, John E.	2nd NC Mtd. Inft.	F	10/01/1863
318	Sentell, William R.	2nd NC Mtd. Inft.	F	10/01/1863
319	Shelton, Roderick	2nd NC Mtd. Inft.	E	09/01/1863
320	Shipman, Alexander F.	2nd NC Mtd. Inft.	B	09/25/1863
321	Shipman, Edward	2nd NC Mtd. Inft.	F	10/01/1863
322	Shipman, James S.	2nd NC Mtd. Inft.	F	10/01/1863
323	Shipman, John M.	2nd NC Mtd. Inft.	B	09/25/1863
324	Sims, Owenby	1st US Vol. Inft.	F	02/24/1864
325	Sluder, James C.	3rd NC Mtd. Inft.	F	10/08/1864
326	Snelson, William R.	3rd NC Mtd. Inft.	I	01/01/1865
327	Snider, Henry J.	6th US Vol. Inft.	F	03/26/1865
328	Sprinkle, David	2nd NC Mtd. Inft.	A	09/15/1863
329	Sprinkle, George	2nd NC Mtd. Inft.	A	09/15/1863
330	Sprinkle, Humphrey	2nd NC Mtd. Inft.	A	09/15/1863
331	Sprinkle, James	2nd NC Mtd. Inft.	A	11/01/1863
332	Sprinkle, Michael	2nd NC Mtd. Inft.	A	09/15/1863
333	Sprinkle, William S.	2nd NC Mtd. Inft.	A	09/15/1863
334	Stanly, William H.	2nd NC Mtd. Inft.	C	01/01/1865
335	Stepp, Henry	2nd NC Mtd. Inft.	B	09/25/1863
336	Stewman, Thomas	1st US Vol. Inft.	F	02/24/1864
337	Stills, George M.	3rd NC Mtd. Inft.	G	09/23/1864
338	Stines, George N.	2nd NC Mtd. Inft.	C	09/26/1863

339	Stines, Joseph E.	2nd NC Mtd. Inft.	C	10/01/1863
340	Stradley, Ebenezer W.	6th US Vol. Inft.	G	03/24/1865
341	Sullivan, Johnathan	3rd NC Mtd. Inft.	I	03/01/1865
342	Suttles, Joseph	2nd NC Mtd. Inft.	D	10/03/1863
343	Swangim, William N.	2nd NC Mtd. Inft.	B	09/25/1863
344	Tabor, Govan	2nd NC Mtd. Inft.	B	09/25/1863
345	Taylor, Samuel J.	2nd NC Mtd. Inft.	A	09/15/1863
346	Thomas, John	2nd NC Mtd. Inft.	A	06/15/1864
347	Tow, Shaderack	3rd NC Mtd. Inft.	C	05/25/1864
348	Townsend, John G.	13th TN Cav.	F	10/01/1864
349	Trantham, Merritt C.	5th US Vol. Inft.	F	04/06/1865
350	Treadway, James	2nd NC Mtd. Inft.	A	09/15/1863
351	Treadway, John	2nd NC Mtd. Inft.	A	09/15/1863
352	Tweed, Albert	2nd NC Mtd. Inft.	E	09/01/1863
353	Vick, Robert C.	5th US Vol. Inft.	?	12/22/1864
354	Waggoner, Adam	2nd NC Mtd. Inft.	A	03/27/1865
355	Waldrop, John	2nd NC Mtd. Inft.	A	09/15/1863
356	Ward, John	2nd NC Mtd. Inft.	B	01/15/1864
357	Ward, William N.	2nd NC Mtd. Inft.	B	09/15/1863
358	Weese, William	2nd NC Mtd. Inft.	F	11/21/1863
359	West, Andrew Jackson	2nd NC Mtd. Inft.	A	09/15/1863
360	West, George W.	2nd NC Mtd. Inft.	A	09/15/1863
361	West, John	2nd NC Mtd. Inft.	B	09/15/1863
362	West, John P.	2nd NC Mtd. Inft.	B	09/25/1863
363	West, Leonard	3rd NC Mtd. Inft.	C	09/26/1864
364	West, Marcus	2nd NC Mtd. Inft.	B	05/01/1864
365	West, William B.	2nd NC Mtd. Inft.	A	04/01/1864
366	West, William P.	3rd NC Mtd. Inft.	C	11/11/1864
367	Whitaker, Solomon	3rd NC Mtd. Inft.	I	03/01/1865
368	White, Henry A.	2nd NC Mtd. Inft.	B	10/01/1863
369	White, James	2nd NC Mtd. Inft.	A	09/15/1863

370	White, Jefferson	2nd NC Mtd. Inft.	A	09/15/1863
371	White, Pharoah	US Navy		06/10/1864
372	White, William	2nd NC Mtd. Inft.	A	02/01/1865
373	Whitmore, Columbus C.	3rd NC Mtd. Inft.	K	03/01/1865
374	Wilds, John H.	2nd NC Mtd. Inft.	C	09/26/1863
375	Wilds, Robert	2nd NC Mtd. Inft.	B	10/01/1863
376	Williams, John H.	3rd NC Mtd. Inft.	K	03/01/1865
377	Wilson, Harrison	6th US Vol. Inft.	D	03/24/1865
378	Wolf, Elbert S.	2nd NC Mtd. Inft.	B	11/04/1864
379	Woodson, Francis Marion	2nd NC Mtd. Inft.	A	09/15/1863
380	Woody, Green	2nd NC Mtd. Inft.	D	10/11/1863
381	Worley, Joseph D.	3rd NC Mtd. Inft.	C	09/23/1864
382	Worley, Wiley J.	3rd NC Mtd. Inft.	G	12/01/1864
383	Wright, James M.	6th US Vol. Inft.	H	03/29/1865
384	Wright, Leander	2nd NC Mtd. Inft.	A	05/01/1864
385	Wright, Monteville	3rd NC Mtd. Inft.	I	03/01/1865
386	Wright, Thomas J.	2nd NC Mtd. Inft.	B	09/25/1863
387	Wright, William T.	3rd NC Mtd. Inft.	C	10/25/1864
388	Wyatt, Alfred J.	3rd NC Mtd. Inft.	D	08/12/1864
389	Young, Lynch	2nd NC Mtd. Inft.	H	10/01/1863

BURKE COUNTY UNION SOLDIERS

	Name	Regiment	Company	Date of Enlistment
1	Bean, Enoch	2nd NC Mtd. Inft.	D	04/15/1865
2	Benfield, Marion	2nd NC Mtd. Inft.	H	10/01/1863
3	Bird, William	2nd NC Mtd. Inft.	D	10/01/1863
4	Burns, Phillip	1st US Vol. Inft.	D	01/24/1864
5	Burton, Aaron J.	3rd NC Mtd. Inft.	G	12/01/1864
6	Butler, John	US Navy		01/23/1864
7	Cloud, Terrell	13th TN Cav.	C	09/01/1865
8	Cook, Thomas	1st US Vol. Inft.	E	02/19/1864
9	Epley, Andrew	US Navy		01/23/1864
10	Franklin, Joseph	3rd NC Mtd. Inft.	A	06/01/1864
11	Griffin, James	3rd MD Cav.	H	08/01/1863
12	Hoppis, Alex	3rd NC Mtd. Inft.	A	07/02/1864
13	Huskins, Jubal	3rd NC Mtd. Inft.	A	03/10/1864
14	Huskins, William C.	3rd NC Mtd. Inft.	A	03/10/1864
15	Johnson, David H.	1st US Vol. Inft.	C	01/29/1864
16	Lane, Jacob	1st US Vol. Inft.	E	02/19/1864
17	Loftus, John H.	2nd NC Mtd. Inft.	B	10/01/1863
18	McFall, Abraham	3rd NC Mtd. Inft.	A	06/01/1864
19	Mitchell, Berry	3rd NC Mtd. Inft.	B	06/19/1864
20	Morgan, Pinkney A.	1st US Vol. Inft.	E	02/19/1864
21	Mull, Henry	1st US Vol. Inft.	C	01/25/1864
22	Pritchard, Adolphus	3rd NC Mtd. Inft.	F	10/05/1864
23	Smith, Ransom	1st CT Cav.	G	10/04/1863
24	Stamey, Martin V.	3rd NC Mtd. Inft.	H	01/25/1865
25	Stansberry, Solomon	13th TN Cav.	K	08/10/1863
26	Stout, Andrew	13th TN Cav.	G	11/01/1864
27	Waycaster, Stephen	2nd NC Mtd. Inft.	A	10/01/1863
28	Wilson, William F.	3rd NC Mtd. Inft.	E	03/25/1864

CALDWELL COUNTY UNION SOLDIERS

	Name	Regiment	Company	Date of Enlistment
1	Bean, Thomas	2nd NC Mtd. Inft.	D	03/10/1865
2	Bean, William W.	2nd NC Mtd. Inft.	D	04/15/1865
3	Carpenter, Albert E.	3rd NC Mtd. Inft.	F	10/05/1864
4	Clark, Adolphus	3rd NC Mtd. Inft.	F	10/05/1864
5	Clark, Detroit	3rd NC Mtd. Inft.	F	10/05/1864
6	Clark, Noah	2nd NC Mtd. Inft.	D	04/15/1865
7	Clark, Thaddeus W.	3rd NC Mtd. Inft.	F	10/05/1864
8	Cobb, Newton	9th TN Cav.	?	?
9	Coffey, Larkin	1st US Vol. Inft.	I	01/29/1864
10	Collins, Solomon	3rd NC Mtd. Inft.	A	06/11/1864
11	Crump, George W.	2nd NC Mtd. Inft.	E	03/10/1865
12	Crump, Henry	2nd NC Mtd. Inft.	E	04/15/1865
13	Curtis, Joshua C.	1st US Vol. Inft.	C	01/26/1864
14	Day, William D.	2nd NC Mtd. Inft.	H	04/15/1865
15	Dinkins, Lewis M.	1st US Vol. Inft.	G	02/10/1864
16	Estes, William	2nd NC Mtd. Inft.	D	04/15/1865
17	Farmer, John R.	13th TN Cav.	E	09/24/1863
18	Gragg, Taylor	2nd NC Mtd. Inft.	E	04/15/1865
19	Green, William H.	1st US Vol. Inft.	A	02/10/1864
20	Greene, Henry	2nd NC Mtd. Inft.	E	03/10/1865
21	Harrison, Joseph E.	3rd NC Mtd. Inft.	H	02/01/1864
22	Hartley, Lewis	2nd NC Mtd. Inft.	B	04/15/1865
23	Hawkins, Jesse D.	3rd US Vol. Inft.	G	10/18/1864
24	Hobbs, Calib A.	6th US Vol. Inft.	G	03/24/1865
25	Hollifield, William H.	3rd NC Mtd. Inft.	A	06/11/1864
26	Horton, John	3rd NC Mtd. Inft.	F	11/01/1864
27	Howell, James H.	5th US Vol. Inft.	F	11/01/1864
28	Jackson, Squire P.	2nd NC Mtd. Inft.	D	03/10/1865

29	Kerby, James M.	2nd NC Mtd. Inft.	B	03/01/1865
30	Moody, Francis	13th TN Cav.	A	09/22/1863
31	Palmer, Joseph M.	1st US Vol. Inft.	K	06/04/1864
32	Pearce, Redmond T.	3rd US Vol. Inft.	G	06/18/1864
33	Pendley, Sidney E.	2nd NC Mtd. Inft.	D	04/15/1865
34	Pendley, Silas J.	2nd NC Mtd. Inft.	D	04/15/1865
35	Philyan, Gideon	2nd NC Mtd. Inft.	D	04/15/1865
36	Prestwood, Luther M.	1st US Vol. Inft.	D	02/10/1864
37	Setser, John H.	2nd NC Mtd. Inft.	D	04/15/1865
38	Sherrill, C. Elisha	1st US Vol. Inft.	D	01/25/1864
39	Simms, James	3rd NC Mtd. Inft.	D	08/06/1864
40	Small, Jesse	4th US Vol. Inft.	C	10/17/1864
41	Small, Kelly	1st US Vol. Inft.	D	01/28/1864
42	Stanton, William	13th TN Cav.	E	09/24/1863
43	Teague, James I.	3rd NC Mtd. Inft.	F	10/05/1864
44	Teague, Nathan A.	1st US Vol. Inft.	K	06/27/1864
45	Thompson, John H.	2nd NC Mtd. Inft.	F	03/01/1865
46	Watson, Henry Eli	3rd US Vol. Inft.	G	10/18/1864
47	Watson, Noah	6th US Vol. Inft.	G	03/24/1865
48	Watson, Tilingham H.	1st US Vol. Inft.	D	01/29/1864
49	Watts, Manly C.	1st US Vol. Inft.	F	02/10/1864
50	Webb, John Calvin	2nd NC Mtd. Inft.	B	04/15/1865
51	White, Joseph H.	2nd NC Mtd. Inft.	D	04/15/1865

CATAWBA COUNTY UNION SOLDIERS

	Name	Regiment	Company	Date of Enlistment
1	Brown, Thomas G.	?	?	10/17/1864
2	Carpenter, Joshua	13th TN Cav.	I	03/01/1864
3	Harmon, David A.	3rd NC Mtd. Inft.	B	07/24/1864
4	Harmon, Lawson	3rd NC Mtd. Inft.	B	07/24/1864
5	Harmon, Will M.	3rd NC Mtd. Inft.	B	07/24/1864
6	Hoover, Jefferson	1st US Vol. Inft.	G	08/30/1863
7	Johnson, Allen Richard	1st US Vol. Inft.	B	01/24/1864
8	Sherrill, Joseph H.	1st US Vol. Inft.	A	01/22/1864
9	Smith, John H.	1st US Vol. Inft.	B	01/29/1864
10	Wade, William	1st US Vol. Inft.	G	06/25/1864

CHEROKEE COUNTY UNION SOLDIERS

	Name	Regiment	Company	Date of Enlistment
1	Barrett, George	2nd NC Mtd. Inft.	D	10/01/1863
2	Brown, Ben	3rd NC Mtd. Inft.	D	06/11/1864
3	Brown, Isaac	3rd NC Mtd. Inft.	D	06/11/1864
4	Burgess, James M.	6th US Vol. Inft.	A	03/16/1865
5	Chio-e-li (Native American)	3rd NC Mtd. Inft.	D	06/11/1864
6	Du-Las-Ki (Native American)	3rd NC Mtd. Inft.	D	06/11/1864
7	Folder, John	3rd NC Mtd. Inft.	D	06/11/1864
8	Hartness, Henry L.	6th IN Cav.	C	08/15/1863
9	Hartness, Thomas	6th IN Cav.	C	08/15/1863
10	Henson, Anderson	2nd NC Mtd. Inft.	D	10/03/1863
11	Henson, James	2nd NC Mtd. Inft.	D	10/03/1863
12	Horton, Almarine H.	6th US Vol. Inft.	G	03/24/1865
13	John (Native American)	3rd NC Mtd. Inft.	B	06/11/1864
14	John Di-A (Native American)	3rd NC Mtd. Inft.	D	06/11/1864
15	John-I-Got-Pa (Native American)	3rd NC Mtd. Inft.	D	06/11/1864
16	Johnson, Stephen	3rd NC Mtd. Inft.	D	06/11/1864
17	Kanot, John	3rd NC Mtd. Inft.	D	06/11/1864
18	Kanot, Thomas	3rd NC Mtd. Inft.	D	06/11/1864
19	Konk-as-ke (Native American)	3rd NC Mtd. Inft.	D	06/11/1864
20	Leadford, Center	2nd NC Mtd. Inft.	D	10/03/1863
21	Leadford, Elisha M.	2nd NC Mtd. Inft.	D	10/03/1863
22	Leadford, James L.	2nd NC Mtd. Inft.	D	10/03/1863
23	Leadford, Jason	2nd NC Mtd. Inft.	D	10/03/1863
24	Leadford, Julius	2nd NC Mtd. Inft.	D	10/03/1863
25	Ledford, David	2nd NC Mtd. Inft.	D	10/11/1863
26	Ledford, William C.	2nd NC Mtd. Inft.	D	10/03/1863
27	McGee, James F.	2nd NC Mtd. Inft.	D	03/10/1865
28	Oter, James (Native American)	3rd NC Mtd. Inft.	D	06/11/1864
29	Palle, David (Native American)	3rd NC Mtd. Inft.	D	06/11/1864

30	Patterson, William A.	2nd NC Mtd. Inft.	D	10/03/1863
31	Plemmons, Adolphus H., Jr.	5th US Vol. Inft.	F	04/01/1865
32	Ratcliff, Mason	3rd NC Mtd. Inft.	D	06/11/1864
33	Ray, Joseph	3rd NC Mtd. Inft.	H	01/15/1865
34	Slu-Na-Na (Native American)	3rd NC Mtd. Inft.	D	06/11/1864
35	Squirrel, Souquilla (Native American)	3rd NC Mtd. Inft.	D	06/11/1864
36	Tah-Li (Native American)	3rd NC Mtd. Inft.	D	06/11/1864
37	Te-Ke-How-Gous-Ki (Native American)	3rd NC Mtd. Inft.	D	06/11/1864
38	Tipton, David	3rd NC Mtd. Inft.	D	07/11/1864
39	Trull, William A.	3rd NC Mtd. Inft.	H	12/01/1864
40	Vi-Na-Der (Native American)	3rd NC Mtd. Inft.	D	06/11/1864
41	Wai-Le (Native American)	3rd NC Mtd. Inft.	D	06/11/1864
42	Walker, John	3rd NC Mtd. Inft.	D	06/11/1864
43	Washington (Native American)	3rd NC Mtd. Inft.	D	06/11/1864
44	Wilson, James	2nd NC Mtd. Inft.	D	10/01/1863
45	Wy-An-Is-Te (Native American)	3rd NC Mtd. Inft.	D	06/11/1864
46	You-Lak-Da (Native American)	3rd NC Mtd. Inft.	D	06/11/1864

CLAY COUNTY UNION SOLDIERS

	Name	*Regiment*	*Company*	*Date of Enlistment*
1	Ditmore, Francis M.	20th KY Inft.	D	12/26/1865
2	Fullbright, Miles F.	3rd US Vol. Inft.	I	10/31/1864
3	Haney, William T.	US Navy		05/25/1864
4	Moses, David	13th TN Cav.	C	08/31/1865
5	Roland, James W.	6th IN Cav.	E	09/01/1863
6	Stamey, Jacob H.	5th US Vol. Inft.	H	04/14/1865
7	Wooten, Thomas K. F.	5th US Vol. Inft.	H	04/14/1865

CLEVELAND COUNTY UNION SOLDIERS

	Name	*Regiment*	*Company*	*Date of Enlistment*
1	Allen, Perry	4th US Vol. Inft.	C	10/15/1864
2	Bigham, William P.	1st US Vol. Inft.	D	02/09/1864
3	Elmore, William	1st US Vol. Inft.	G	01/30/1864
4	Harden, George W.	Ahl's DE Heavy Art.		07/27/1863
5	Hoyle, Joel	1st US Vol. Inft.	C	01/29/1864
6	Kiser, Robert G.	1st US Vol. Inft.	K	06/24/1864
7	Long, William	1st US Vol. Inft.	C	01/26/1864
8	Martin, James P.	1st US Vol. Inft.	F	02/25/1864
9	Neal, J. Marion	1st US Vol. Inft.	G	01/26/1864
10	Pryor, Robert Pinkney	4th US Vol. Inft.	C	08/24/1864
11	Ravel, Henry B.	1st US Vol. Inft.	A	01/26/1864
12	Swafford, James	13th TN Cav.	C	03/20/1865

HAYWOOD COUNTY UNION SOLDIERS

	Name	Regiment	Company	Date of Enlistment
1	Arbury, Niner A.	3rd NC Mtd. Inft.	H	01/25/1865
2	Branum, Marion	2nd TN Cav.	I	10/31/1862
3	Burgess, Aden H.	2nd NC Mtd. Inft.	E	09/01/1863
4	Caldwell, Andrew	3rd NC Mtd. Inft.	H	01/25/1865
5	Caldwell, David M.	3rd NC Mtd. Inft.	H	01/25/1865
6	Caldwell, Hamilton	3rd NC Mtd. Inft.	H	01/25/1865
7	Chambers, Asia C.	3rd NC Mtd. Inft.	I	03/01/1865
8	Clark, Richard M.	3rd NC Mtd. Inft.	H	10/08/1864
9	Cooper, Lina	3rd NC Mtd. Inft.	H	02/16/1865
10	Craig, Drewry	3rd NC Mtd. Inft.	H	01/15/1865
11	Grooms, George, Jr.	11th TN Cav.	?	10/16/1863
12	Grooms, John	11th TN Cav.	?	10/16/1863
13	Guinn, Jackson	20th KY Inft.	G	09/24/1863
14	Hall, George	3rd NC Mtd. Inft.	H	01/25/1865
15	Hall, Leander	3rd NC Mtd. Inft.	H	01/25/1865
16	Harbin, David T.	3rd NC Mtd. Inft.	C	10/08/1864
17	Harbin, Oliver N.	2nd NC Mtd. Inft.	F	11/01/1863
18	Hill, Riley	3rd NC Mtd. Inft.	C	09/26/1864
19	Man, Andrew	13th TN Cav.	M	02/02/1864
20	Martin, Albert	2nd NC Mtd. Inft.	D	10/03/1863
21	McCracken, William H.	5th US Vol. Inft.	H	04/14/1865
22	McIntire, Zachary	2nd NC Mtd. Inft.	B	05/01/1864
23	Mull, Leander	3rd NC Mtd. Inft.	H	01/05/1865
24	Mull, William E.	2nd NC Mtd. Inft.	D	04/14/1864
25	Penland, Hiram	3rd NC Mtd. Inft.	H	01/25/1865
26	Queen, Robert T.	5th US Vol. Inft.	?	04/14/1865
27	Roberson, Richard, Sr.	8th TN Cav.	L	10/01/1863
28	Roberts, Elisha	2nd NC Mtd. Inft.	D	10/03/1863
29	Roberts, William	2nd NC Mtd. Inft.	D	10/11/1863
30	Vess, David M.	8th TN Cav.	E	?
31	Williams, Robert P.	3rd NC Mtd. Inft.	G	01/15/1865

HENDERSON COUNTY UNION SOLDIERS

	Name	Regiment	Company	Date of Enlistment
1	Allen, John	2nd NC Mtd. Inft.	F	11/21/1863
2	Arthurburn, Isaac	US Navy		12/31/1863
3	Blackwell, Francis M.	2nd NC Mtd. Inft.	B	09/25/1863
4	Blackwell, John	2nd NC Mtd. Inft.	B	09/25/1863
5	Blackwell, Thomas	2nd NC Mtd. Inft.	B	09/25/1863
6	Cagel, James H.	2nd NC Mtd. Inft.	F	11/21/1863
7	Cagle, James H.	3rd NC Mtd. Inft.	D	10/08/1864
8	Cairn, William H.	3rd NC Mtd. Inft.	A	06/14/1864
9	Capps, William	3rd NC Mtd. Inft.	C	10/10/1864
10	Capps, William M.	3rd NC Mtd. Inft.	H	01/15/1865
11	Carttrell, Valentine	2nd NC Mtd. Inft.	F	10/01/1863
12	Carup, James I.	2nd NC Mtd. Inft.	F	10/01/1863
13	Cass, Allen R.	3rd NC Mtd. Inft.	E	03/16/1864
14	Citton, Silas C.	3rd NC Mtd. Inft.	I	03/01/1865
15	Clark, William H.	2nd NC Mtd. Inft.	H	11/01/1864
16	Condrey, Gilford J.	1st US Vol. Inft.	C	06/22/1864
17	Corn, Ezekiel W.	1st US Vol. Inft.	H	05/17/1864
18	Cross, Joseph	3rd NC Mtd. Inft.	H	01/16/1865
19	Drake, Hezekiah	2nd NC Mtd. Inft.	C	10/01/1863
20	Drake, John B.	2nd NC Mtd. Inft.	C	10/01/1863
21	Drake, John H.	2nd NC Mtd. Inft.	F	10/01/1863
22	Drake, Nathan M.	2nd NC Mtd. Inft.	B	10/01/1863
23	Drake, Richard	2nd NC Mtd. Inft.	C	10/01/1863
24	Drake, William	2nd NC Mtd. Inft.	F	10/01/1863
25	Ensley, Elijah L.	2nd NC Mtd. Inft.	F	10/01/1863
26	Evans, James L.	2nd NC Mtd. Inft.	C	09/26/1863
27	Fowler, John M.	3rd NC Mtd. Inft.	A	06/11/1864
28	Fowler, Martin	3rd NC Mtd. Inft.	I	03/06/1865

29	Fullam, Albert W.	3rd NC Mtd. Inft.	C	09/25/1864
30	Galloway, Albert L.	3rd NC Mtd. Inft.	D	09/18/1864
31	Galloway, Merritt H.	3rd NC Mtd. Inft.	E	03/16/1864
32	Garren, Anderson	3rd NC Mtd. Inft.	E	10/16/1864
33	Garren, Mitchell	3rd NC Mtd. Inft.	E	09/18/1864
34	Gilbert, Daniel	2nd NC Mtd. Inft.	B	09/25/1863
35	Gilreath, Mason	3rd NC Mtd. Inft.	I	03/01/1865
36	Hamilton, Solomon W.	2nd NC Mtd. Inft.	F	10/01/1863
37	Hammit, James V.	US Navy		01/25/1864
38	Hammons, James	2nd NC Mtd. Inft.	H	10/01/1863
39	Heatherly, David	2nd NC Mtd. Inft.	A	09/15/1864
40	Heatherly, Merritt R.	2nd NC Mtd. Inft.	H	10/01/1863
41	Henderson, Benjamin F.	3rd NC Mtd. Inft.	C	09/17/1864
42	Henderson, George	3rd NC Mtd. Inft.	H	01/01/1865
43	Henderson, Hensley	3rd NC Mtd. Inft.	I	02/01/1865
44	Henderson, William H.	3rd NC Mtd. Inft.	C	09/17/1864
45	Henderson, William M.	2nd NC Mtd. Inft.	F	10/01/1863
46	Hood, Perry Newton	2nd US Vol. Inft.	G	10/06/1864
47	Huggins, Odious M.	2nd NC Mtd. Inft.	B	10/01/1865
48	Jones, Hezekiah	2nd NC Mtd. Inft.	C	10/01/1863
49	Jones, Hicks	2nd NC Mtd. Inft.	H	10/01/1863
50	Jones, Hiram K.	2nd NC Mtd. Inft.	H	10/06/1864
51	Jones, James	2nd NC Mtd. Inft.	H	05/06/1864
52	Jones, John	2nd NC Mtd. Inft.	B	09/25/1863
53	Jones, Robert Jr.	2nd NC Mtd. Inft.	H	05/06/1864
54	Jones, Robert Sr.	2nd NC Mtd. Inft.	B	09/25/1863
55	Jones, Solomon	2nd NC Mtd. Inft.	C	10/01/1863
56	Jones, Thomas	2nd NC Mtd. Inft.	D	04/15/1865
57	Justice, Joshua F.	2nd NC Mtd. Inft.	H	10/01/1863
58	Justus, Jesse R.	2nd NC Mtd. Inft.	H	11/04/1864
59	Justus, William R.	2nd NC Mtd. Inft.	H	09/25/1863

60	Kennemore, Charles W.	3rd NC Mtd. Inft.	C	09/17/1864
61	Kennemore, John R.	3rd NC Mtd. Inft.	C	09/17/1864
62	Kilpatrick, William P.	2nd NC Mtd. Inft.	F	10/01/1863
63	Kirkendall, Ezekiel	2nd NC Mtd. Inft.	C	09/26/1863
64	Kirkendall, Joseph	2nd NC Mtd. Inft.	B	09/25/1863
65	Kitchen, Jason	2nd NC Mtd. Inft.	F	10/01/1863
66	Kuykendall, Alfred	2nd NC Mtd. Inft.	H	10/01/1863
67	Lanning, Andrew J.	2nd NC Mtd. Inft.	F	10/01/1863
68	Lanning, William C.	2nd NC Mtd. Inft.	F	10/01/1863
69	Lanning, William C.	3rd NC Mtd. Inft.	I	10/20/1864
70	Leveritt, Jesse L.	2nd NC Mtd. Inft.	H	10/01/1863
71	Lofton, Harison A.	4th US Vol. Inft.	B	10/15/1864
72	Loftus, Kosea D.	2nd NC Mtd. Inft.	F	10/01/1863
73	Marshal, Thomas	2nd NC Mtd. Inft.	H	10/01/1863
74	McCall, Alexander G.	2nd NC Mtd. Inft.	F	10/01/1863
75	McCall, John A.	2nd NC Mtd. Inft.	F	10/01/1863
76	McClain, Rufus T.	3rd NC Mtd. Inft.	I	03/01/1865
77	McCrary, Adolphus	2nd NC Mtd. Inft.	H	11/01/1863
78	McGaha, William H.	2nd NC Mtd. Inft.	F	10/01/1863
79	Merrell, Perry	2nd NC Mtd. Inft.	F	10/01/1863
80	Merrell, Samuel	2nd NC Mtd. Inft.	F	03/30/1865
81	Merrell, William F.	2nd NC Mtd. Inft.	F	03/30/1865
82	Moore, Hezekiah P.	2nd NC Mtd. Inft.	F	10/01/1863
83	Moore, William R.	2nd NC Mtd. Inft.	F	10/01/1863
84	Morrison, David M.	2nd NC Mtd. Inft.	B	09/25/1863
85	Nelson, Elisha K.	3rd NC Mtd. Inft.	F	08/06/1864
86	Orr, George L.	2nd NC Mtd. Inft.	F	10/01/1863
87	Orr, Robert F.	2nd NC Mtd. Inft.	F	10/01/1863
88	Osteen, Calvin	2nd NC Mtd. Inft.	B	10/01/1863
89	Osteen, John C.	2nd NC Mtd. Inft.	F	10/01/1863
90	Osteen, Luke	2nd NC Mtd. Inft.	B	10/01/1864

91	Osteen, Richard S.	2nd NC Mtd. Inft.	F	03/01/1865
92	Osteen, Robert V.	2nd NC Mtd. Inft.	F	03/01/1865
93	Osteen, Solomon D.	2nd NC Mtd. Inft.	B	10/01/1864
94	Owens, John A.	2nd NC Mtd. Inft.	D	10/03/1863
95	Pace, William J.	2nd NC Mtd. Inft.	H	10/01/1863
96	Paris, Henry	2nd NC Mtd. Inft.	H	10/01/1863
97	Patterson, Drewry W.	3rd NC Mtd. Inft.	E	11/06/1864
98	Patton, William L.	6th US Vol. Inft.	I	04/02/1865
99	Pearson, Adolphus A.	2nd NC Mtd. Inft.	F	03/20/1865
100	Reese, Alson E.	3rd NC Mtd. Inft.	A	06/11/1864
101	Rollins, Isaac	6th US Vol. Inft.	I	04/02/1865
102	Shehan, Bynum	2nd NC Mtd. Inft.	H	10/01/1863
103	Shehan, John	2nd NC Mtd. Inft.	H	10/01/1863
104	Shipman, Alexander	2nd NC Mtd. Inft.	F	03/30/1865
105	Shipman, Caleb	2nd NC Mtd. Inft.	F	10/01/1863
106	Shipman, Edmond C.	2nd NC Mtd. Inft.	H	10/01/1863
107	Shipman, Francis A.	2nd NC Mtd. Inft.	B	09/25/1863
108	Shipman, John B.	2nd NC Mtd. Inft.	H	10/01/1863
109	Shipman, Marion P.	2nd NC Mtd. Inft.	B	09/25/1863
110	Shipman, William	2nd NC Mtd. Inft.	F	10/01/1863
111	Smith, John E.	3rd NC Mtd. Inft.	A	06/11/1864
112	Spain, James M.	6th US Vol. Inft.	G	05/22/1864
113	Staton, Jesse A.	2nd NC Mtd. Inft.	H	10/01/1863
114	Stepp, Abraham T.	2nd NC Mtd. Inft.	H	10/01/1863
115	Stepp, Alfred	2nd NC Mtd. Inft.	H	10/01/1863
116	Stepp, Reuben M.	2nd NC Mtd. Inft.	B	09/25/1863
117	Stepp, Robert	2nd NC Mtd. Inft.	H	10/01/1863
118	Stepp, William H.	2nd NC Mtd. Inft.	H	10/01/1863
119	Steward, Melvin M.	3rd NC Mtd. Inft.	I	12/25/1864
120	Stewart, Thomas	2nd NC Mtd. Inft.	F	10/01/1863
121	Swaney, Isham H.	6th US Vol. Inft.	D	12/22/1864

122	Swangim, John	2nd NC Mtd. Inft.	F	10/01/1863
123	Swangin, John B.	3rd NC Mtd. Inft.	B	08/25/1864
124	Taylor, Jeremiah	2nd NC Mtd. Inft.	H	10/01/1863
125	Taylor, Jeremiah M.	3rd NC Mtd. Inft.	E	10/06/1864
126	Taylor, John D.	3rd NC Mtd. Inft.	E	10/06/1864
127	Tow, Samuel M.	US Navy		01/25/1864
128	Walker, Robert D.	2nd NC Mtd. Inft.	B	09/25/1863
129	Watts, Rufus	3rd NC Mtd. Inft.	G	09/12/1864
130	Weese, John	2nd NC Mtd. Inft.	F	10/01/1863

JACKSON COUNTY UNION SOLDIERS

	Name	Regiment	Company	Date of Enlistment
1	Anitso, James	3rd NC Mtd. Inft.	D	11/15/1864
2	Benson, Alexander C.	6th IN Cav.	F	09/01/1863
3	Bradshaw, George	5th US Vol. Inft.	E	04/21/1865
4	Bumgarner, Emos S.	6th IN Cav.	F	09/01/1863
5	Freeman, John A.	6th IN Cav.	F	09/01/1863
6	Henson, William W.	6th US Vol. Inft.	B	05/05/1865
7	Hesterband, John	3rd NC Mtd. Inft.	D	04/20/1864
8	Hooper, Alfred M.	9th TN Cav.	D	06/01/1864
9	Hooper, Henry M.	9th TN Cav.	D	03/09/1864
10	Kanot, Tatageesga	3rd NC Mtd. Inft.	D	11/16/1864
11	Ok-Wa-Taga (Native American)	3rd NC Mtd. Inft.	D	11/15/1864
12	Ool-Ay-Way, Thomas (Native Amer.)	3rd NC Mtd. Inft.	D	11/15/1864
13	Ool-Stoo-Ee, John (Native American)	3rd NC Mtd. Inft.	D	11/15/1864
14	Oter, Thomas (Native American)	3rd NC Mtd. Inft.	D	11/15/1864
15	Owens, Alexander	5th US Vol. Inft.	I	04/15/1865
16	Partridge, Chur (Native American)	3rd NC Mtd. Inft.	D	04/01/1864
17	Partridge, Colsgun (Native Amer.)	3rd NC Mtd. Inft.	D	04/01/1864
18	Seay, James M.	3rd NC Mtd. Inft.	I	02/28/1865
19	Skitta, Mike	3rd NC Mtd. Inft.	D	04/10/1865
20	Sutton, John	3rd NC Mtd. Inft.	D	11/11/1864
21	Townsend, Robert	3rd NC Mtd. Inft.	D	11/10/1864
22	Wadkins, John	3rd NC Mtd. Inft.	D	04/26/1864
23	Walkingstick, James (Native Amer.)	3rd NC Mtd. Inft.	D	02/04/1865
24	Walkingstick, Thomas (Nat. Amer.)	3rd NC Mtd. Inft.	D	02/10/1865
25	Wood, John B.	3rd NC Mtd. Inft.	D	08/01/1864
26	Wood, William J.	3rd NC Mtd. Inft.	D	09/18/1864
27	Woodring, David C.	5th US Vol. Inft.	F	04/24/1865

MACON COUNTY UNION SOLDIERS

	Name	*Regiment*	*Company*	*Date of Enlistment*
1	Arklook, John	3rd NC Mtd. Inft.	D	07/01/1864
2	Benfield, John H.	6th IN Cav.	F	07/13/1863
3	Calloway, William T.	6th US Vol. Inft.	D	05/05/1865
4	Corn, Jessee	2nd NC Mtd. Inft.	D	10/03/1863
5	Deal, Joseph A.	13th TN Cav.	C	02/01/1865
6	Dills, Francis M.	2nd NC Mtd. Inft.	D	10/01/1863
7	Henson, Milton	3rd NC Mtd. Inft.	G	09/01/1864
8	Jondon, Robert	1st US Vol. Inft.	B	01/26/1864
9	Knight, George W.	5th US Vol. Inft.	H	04/14/1865
10	Knight, John L.	3rd MD Cav.	H	08/12/1863
11	Love, William N.	5th US Vol. Inft.	H	04/24/1865
12	Miller, Samuel	2nd NC Mtd. Inft.	C	10/01/1863
13	Nichols, Alexander H.	6th US Vol. Inft.	C	05/05/1865
14	Nichols, Gilbert R.	5th US Vol. Inft.	H	04/24/1865
15	Oliver, John C.	1st US Vol. Inft.	C	02/01/1864
16	Oliver, Madison C.	1st US Vol. Inft.	C	01/26/1864
17	Oliver, William P.	6th US Vol. Inft.	H	03/29/1865
18	Payne, James O.	13th TN Cav.	K	09/23/1863
19	Proctor, James	6th US Vol. Inft.	I	04/02/1865
20	Roberts, Jacob M.	2nd NC Mtd. Inft.	B	09/04/1864
21	Stanfield, Thomas L.	1st US Vol. Inft.	G	01/29/1864
22	Swanger, George W.	6th US Vol. Inft.	I	04/02/1865

MADISON COUNTY UNION SOLDIERS

	Name	Regiment	Company	Date of Enlistment
1	Allen, Avery C.	13th TN Cav.	K	09/24/1863
2	Anderson, James F.	2nd NC Mtd. Inft.	C	01/01/1865
3	Anderson, John T.	3rd NC Mtd. Inft.	B	08/25/1864
4	Anderson, Robert	3rd NC Mtd. Inft.	C	09/01/1864
5	Arrowood, James	2nd NC Mtd. Inft.	A	09/15/1863
6	Austin, William H.	20th KY Inft.	G	09/24/1863
7	Ballard, John P.	4th TN Cav.	K	08/31/1864
8	Banks, John	3rd NC Mtd. Inft.	G	02/20/1865
9	Barnett, John	3rd NC Mtd. Inft.	B	06/26/1864
10	Blankenship, Noah	3rd NC Mtd. Inft.	C	02/20/1865
11	Boon, Thomas	3rd NC Mtd. Inft.	B	03/03/1864
12	Bradburn, William	2nd NC Mtd. Inft.	C	09/26/1863
13	Brooks, Abner	2nd NC Mtd. Inft.	C	9/26/1964
14	Brooks, John	2nd NC Mtd. Inft.	C	9/26/1964
15	Buckner, James R.	3rd NC Mtd. Inft.	G	01/01/1865
16	Caldwell, James	3rd NC Mtd. Inft.	H	01/25/1865
17	Candler, Thomas J.	2nd NC Mtd. Inft.	E	11/16/1864
18	Cody, Gabriel	3rd NC Mtd. Inft.	G	12/01/1864
19	Cody, William	3rd NC Mtd. Inft.	G	12/01/1864
20	Cogdill, William A.	4th US Vol. Inft.	A	10/15/1864
21	Crain, Albert	4th TN Mtd. Inft.	C	?
22	Davis, Andrew Jackson	6th US Vol. Inft.	D	03/24/1865
23	Davis, Nathaniel, Jr.	US Navy		09/09/1863
24	Dockery, Alfred L.	2nd NC Mtd. Inft.	C	09/26/1863
25	Dockery, Franklin	US Navy		12/31/1863
26	Edington, Fowler	2nd NC Mtd. Inft.	E	09/01/1863
27	Edwards, James	3rd NC Mtd. Inft.	I	02/10/1865
28	Elder, Ephraim	3rd NC Mtd. Inft.	C	09/22/1864

29	Freman, David L.	20th KY Inft.	G	09/24/1863
30	Gentry, George W.	2nd NC Mtd. Inft.	E	09/01/1863
31	Gentry, Robert	2nd NC Mtd. Inft.	B	04/01/1864
32	Gentry, William	2nd NC Mtd. Inft.	C	09/26/1863
33	Gillis, Elbert	3rd NC Mtd. Inft.	K	03/01/1865
34	Gillon, Marcus W.	6th US Vol. Inft.	B	03/20/1865
35	Goforth, Ezekiel P.	2nd NC Mtd. Inft.	C	06/29/1864
36	Goforth, Miles	3rd NC Mtd. Inft.	B	08/25/1864
37	Gosnell, Charles	3rd NC Mtd. Inft.	G	10/01/1864
38	Gosnell, James	2nd NC Mtd. Inft.	E	09/01/1863
39	Gosnell, Joeberry	3rd NC Mtd. Inft.	B	06/17/1864
40	Gosnell, Morris	3rd NC Mtd. Inft.	B	06/17/1864
41	Gowin, Daniel H.	?	?	10/18/1864
42	Gregory, Milas L.	3rd NC Mtd. Inft.	K	03/01/1865
43	Gregory, William M.	3rd NC Mtd. Inft.	H	12/27/1864
44	Griffy, James	2nd NC Mtd. Inft.	D	10/01/1863
45	Gunter, Jason R.	2nd NC Mtd. Inft.	E	09/01/1863
46	Gunther, Charles	3rd NC Mtd. Inft.	G	09/12/1864
47	Hair, Henry C.	3rd NC Mtd. Inft.	G	09/23/1864
48	Henderson, John	2nd NC Mtd. Inft.	E	09/15/1864
49	Henderson, Zachariah	2nd NC Mtd. Inft.	H	10/01/1863
50	Hensley, Amos	3rd NC Mtd. Inft.	A	06/01/1864
51	Hensley, Zachariah	2nd NC Mtd. Inft.	E	09/01/1863
52	Hensly, Matthew	3rd NC Mtd. Inft.	G	07/21/1864
53	Henson, Matthew	3rd NC Mtd. Inft.	H	07/21/1864
54	Hill, Aaron L.	1st US Vol. Inft.	I	06/27/1864
55	Holcombe, John	3rd NC Mtd. Inft.	K	03/01/1865
56	Holt, Stephen	3rd NC Mtd. Inft.	H	01/15/1865
57	Lewis, Joseph	2nd NC Mtd. Inft.	B	10/01/1863
58	Loudermilk, John L.	1st US Vol. Inft.	F	06/15/1864
59	McCoy, William J.	2nd NC Mtd. Inft.	E	09/01/1863

60	McLean, Woodfin K.	2nd NC Mtd. Inft.	F	04/01/1864
61	Metcalf, Levi	3rd NC Mtd. Inft.	K	03/01/1865
62	Metcalf, William	3rd NC Mtd. Inft.	I	02/01/1865
63	Moore, J. F.	US Navy		05/27/1864
64	Norton, George, Jr.	2nd NC Mtd. Inft.	E	09/01/1863
65	Norton, George, Sr.	2nd NC Mtd. Inft.	E	09/01/1863
66	Norton, Hackney	2nd NC Mtd. Inft.	E	09/01/1863
67	Norton, James	2nd NC Mtd. Inft.	E	09/01/1863
68	Norton, John	3rd NC Mtd. Inft.	G	09/17/1864
69	Norton, Josiah	3rd NC Mtd. Inft.	A	06/11/1864
70	Norton, Martin	3rd NC Mtd. Inft.	A	06/11/1864
71	Norton, Morris	3rd NC Mtd. Inft.	B	06/17/1864
72	Norton, William	3rd NC Mtd. Inft.	G	09/23/1864
73	Norton, William, Jr.	2nd NC Mtd. Inft.	E	09/01/1863
74	Paris, Levi	3rd NC Mtd. Inft.	C	03/25/1864
75	Payne, Adolphus M.	3rd NC Mtd. Inft.	C	09/12/1864
76	Payne, James	3rd NC Mtd. Inft.	C	09/12/1864
77	Pinion, Andrew	3rd NC Mtd. Inft.	I	02/01/1865
78	Ponder, Robert	3rd NC Mtd. Inft.	C	03/01/1865
79	Ramsey, George	3rd NC Mtd. Inft.	C	08/22/1864
80	Ramsey, James	3rd NC Mtd. Inft.	C	08/22/1864
81	Randall, James Mitchell	20th KY Inft.	G	09/24/1863
82	Ray, James H.	3rd NC Mtd. Inft.	K	03/01/1865
83	Ray, William S.	3rd NC Mtd. Inft.	G	06/01/1864
84	Rector, Elijah	3rd NC Mtd. Inft.	C	08/20/1864
85	Rector, William C.	3rd NC Mtd. Inft.	C	03/05/1865
86	Redman, David	3rd NC Mtd. Inft.	C	03/01/1865
87	Rice, Edmund	3rd NC Mtd. Inft.	A	06/11/1864
88	Rice, Isaac	3rd NC Mtd. Inft.	C	08/24/1864
89	Rice, James	2nd NC Mtd. Inft.	A	04/01/1864
90	Rice, James M.	3rd NC Mtd. Inft.	G	01/01/1865

91	Rice, Thomas	3rd NC Mtd. Inft.	I	02/12/1865
92	Rice, Thomas Shephard	US Navy		12/31/1863
93	Riddle, Hezekiah	3rd NC Mtd. Inft.	A	06/11/1864
94	Ridons, James	US Navy		01/25/1864
95	Rigsbee, William	20th KY Inft.	G	09/24/1863
96	Roberts, Alfred	3rd NC Mtd. Inft.	D	10/08/1864
97	Roberts, Davis	US Navy		09/24/1863
98	Roberts, Martin L.	3rd NC Mtd. Inft.	C	03/25/1864
99	Roberts, Zeb B.	2nd NC Mtd. Inft.	E	08/25/1864
100	Robertson, Samuel C.	3rd NC Mtd. Inft.	C	03/25/1865
101	Robinson, Mitchell E.	2nd NC Mtd. Inft.	B	10/17/1863
102	Rollins, William W.	3rd NC Mtd. Inft.	F	03/14/1865
103	Runnion, Thomas I.	3rd NC Mtd. Inft.	K	03/01/1865
104	Sames, Edward	2nd NC Mtd. Inft.	B	10/01/1863
105	Sams, Asa W.	5th US Vol. Inft.	K	04/18/1865
106	Sams, Gabriel	2nd NC Mtd. Inft.	E	09/01/1863
107	Sams, Gabriel	3rd NC Mtd. Inft.	A	06/11/1864
108	Sams, James R.	5th US Vol. Inft.	K	04/24/1865
109	Sams, William Washington	US Navy		01/31/1864
110	Sanders, J. S.	US Navy		01/25/1864
111	Shelton, Andrew J.	3rd NC Mtd. Inft.	G	03/25/1864
112	Shelton, Christopher C.	2nd NC Mtd. Inft.	E	09/01/1863
113	Shelton, Clingman	2nd NC Mtd. Inft.	E	09/01/1863
114	Shelton, David	3rd NC Mtd. Inft.	G	05/16/1864
115	Shelton, Elifuse	3rd NC Mtd. Inft.	G	05/15/1864
116	Shelton, Eliphus	2nd NC Mtd. Inft.	E	09/01/1863
117	Shelton, Isaac	2nd NC Mtd. Inft.	E	09/01/1863
118	Shelton, James	3rd NC Mtd. Inft.	G	06/01/1864
119	Stockton, Francis M.	3rd NC Mtd. Inft.	K	03/01/1865
120	Taylor, John	2nd NC Mtd. Inft.	E	09/01/1863

121	Teague, Edward	3rd NC Mtd. Inft.	C	03/01/1865
122	Thomas, Peter	5th US Vol. Inft.	H	04/14/1865
123	Waddell, Russel	2nd NC Mtd. Inft.	D	10/01/1863
124	Waddell, Samuel	2nd NC Mtd. Inft.	D	10/01/1863
125	Waldrop, William	3rd NC Mtd. Inft.	G	02/12/1865
126	Watts, William	3rd NC Mtd. Inft.	A	06/11/1864
127	West, William L.	3rd NC Mtd. Inft.	C	03/25/1864
128	West, Zachariah	6th US Vol. Inft.	D	03/24/1865
129	Wilds, Jacob H.	3rd NC Mtd. Inft.	A	06/11/1864
130	Wilds, John M.	3rd NC Mtd. Inft.	A	06/11/1864
131	Willis, John A.	6th US Vol. Inft.	D	03/24/1865
132	Willson, Michael	3rd NC Mtd. Inft.	C	03/01/1865
133	Worley, Henry	3rd NC Mtd. Inft.	C	09/12/1864
134	Wright, John W.	6th US Vol. Inft.	F	03/26/1865
135	Young, Clinton E.	13th TN Cav.	K	09/24/1863

McDOWELL COUNTY UNION SOLDIERS

	Name	*Regiment*	*Company*	*Date of Enlistment*
1	Bailey, Jasper S.	3rd NC Mtd. Inft.	D	08/10/1864
2	Ballew, John	3rd NC Mtd. Inft.	A	06/11/1864
3	Bradley, Thomas	2nd NC Mtd. Inft.	H	10/01/1863
4	Bradshaw, William	3rd NC Mtd. Inft.	A	06/11/1864
5	Butler, William	13th TN Cav.	B	09/23/1863
6	Carver, James H.	13th TN Cav.	B	09/23/1863
7	Carver, John	13th TN Cav.	B	09/23/1863
8	Carver, John W.	13th TN Cav.	C	02/01/1865
9	Creswell, Francis M.	1st US Vol. Inft.	D	06/20/1864
10	Dalton, James A.	3rd NC Mtd. Inft.	D	09/12/1864
11	Davis, Reuben	2nd NC Mtd. Inft.	H	10/01/1863
12	Davis, Robert A.	2nd NC Mtd. Inft.	H	10/01/1863
13	Davis, Silas	2nd NC Mtd. Inft.	H	10/01/1863
14	Davis, Thomas M.	2nd NC Mtd. Inft.	H	10/01/1863
15	Dickson, Charles R.	13th TN Cav.	?	02/01/1865
16	England, David R.	2nd NC Mtd. Inft.	H	10/01/1863
17	Fortune, Walter A.	2nd NC Mtd. Inft.	B	09/25/1863
18	Goforth, Miles A.	2nd NC Mtd. Inft.	C	09/26/1863
19	Good, William J.	3rd NC Mtd. Inft.	A	08/15/1864
20	Harris, John C.	1st US Vol. Inft.	D	02/05/1864
21	Haynes, Edward A.	?	?	06/04/1864
22	Haynie, James M.	2nd NC Mtd. Inft.	A	09/15/1863
23	Haynie, John	2nd NC Mtd. Inft.	A	09/15/1863
24	Haynie, William G.	2nd NC Mtd. Inft.	A	09/15/1863
25	Hopson, William	13th TN Cav.	B	10/28/1863
26	Houghstetler, J. B.	4th US Vol. Inft.	C	10/15/1864
27	Hudgins, Andrew J.	6th US Vol. Inft.	D	03/24/1865
28	Jamison, James P.	1st US Vol. Inft.	G	02/05/1864
29	Jaynes, Burgess G.	1st US Vol. Inft.	C	01/29/1864

30	Leakey, John S.	2nd NC Mtd. Inft.	H	12/20/1864
31	Leaky, Henry	13th TN Cav.	K	12/01/1864
32	Matthews, Henry Calvin	3rd NC Mtd. Inft.	A	06/11/1864
33	McCoy, Daniel M.	1st US Vol. Inft.	I	05/30/1864
34	McKinney, Waitstel	13th TN Cav.	C	09/01/1865
35	Moody, William H.	4th US Vol. Inft.	B	10/15/1864
36	Neasbill, Thomas L.	2nd NC Mtd. Inft.	H	12/20/1864
37	Odear, William H.	1st US Vol. Inft.	H	05/17/1864
38	Quinn, Joseph	1st US Vol. Inft.	D	02/05/1864
39	Shehan, James E.	3rd NC Mtd. Inft.	A	06/11/1864
40	Simmons, Leander	3rd NC Mtd. Inft.	A	06/11/1864
41	Smith, William	2nd NC Mtd. Inft.	E	03/10/1865
42	Smith, William S.	1st US Vol. Inft.	K	06/04/1864
43	Walker, Jonathan C.	2nd NC Mtd. Inft.	D	10/11/1863
44	Watts, William	13th TN Cav.	E	10/01/1863

MITCHELL COUNTY UNION SOLDIERS

	Name	Regiment	Company	Date of Enlistment
1	Aldridge, Waitstel	13th TN Cav.	C	11/21/1863
2	Arrowood, Wesley	13th TN Cav.	C	10/28/1863
3	Barnett, John	3rd NC Mtd. Inft.	E	03/25/1864
4	Black, William	13th TN Cav.	C	09/24/1863
5	Buchanan, Alexander	13th TN Cav.	C	01/24/1864
6	Buchanan, Caley	13th TN Cav.	C	09/24/1863
7	Buchanan, David M.	13th TN Cav.	C	01/14/1864
8	Buchanan, Green	3rd NC Mtd. Inft.	E	03/25/1865
9	Buchanan, Joseph	13th TN Cav.	C	10/02/1864
10	Buchanan, Joseph M.	13th TN Cav.	C	09/24/1863
11	Buchanan, William	13th TN Cav.	C	01/14/1864
12	Buchanan, William A.	3rd NC Mtd. Inft.	E	03/25/1865
13	Burleson, Greenberg	13th TN Cav.	B	09/23/1863
14	Burleson, Oliver	13th TN Cav.	B	09/23/1863
15	Burleson, William	13th TN Cav.	C	01/14/1864
16	Burris, James	13th TN Cav.	C	09/24/1863
17	Butler, Alan	US Navy		01/25/1864
18	Byrd, Carson	13th TN Cav.	B	07/24/1863
19	Calloway, William	13th TN Cav.	C	09/26/1863
20	Carpenter, Jonathan	3rd NC Mtd. Inft.	F	10/05/1864
21	Coffey, Jesse Patterson	1st US Vol. Inft.	D	06/27/1864
22	Davis, Josiah	3rd NC Mtd. Inft.	E	03/25/1864
23	Estes, Samuel	3rd NC Mtd. Inft.	K	03/01/1865
24	Foster, Joseph	13th TN Cav.	C	01/26/1864
25	Franklin, James	2nd NC Mtd. Inft.	E	04/15/1865
26	Franklin, Levi A.	13th TN Cav.	C	09/24/1863
27	Frazier, John W.	13th TN Cav.	B	09/05/1863
28	Garland, Charles	3rd NC Mtd. Inft.	H	10/01/1864
29	Garland, Christopher R.	13th TN Cav.	B	09/23/1864

30	Garland, David	13th TN Cav.	B	10/28/1863
31	Garland, Elisha	13th TN Cav.	B	05/11/1864
32	Garland, Ezekial	3rd NC Mtd. Inft.	E	03/25/1864
33	Garland, James B.	13th TN Cav.	B	09/23/1864
34	Garland, John	3rd NC Mtd. Inft.	E	03/25/1864
35	Garland, Joseph E.	13th TN Cav.	M	09/03/1864
36	Garland, Samuel	3rd NC Mtd. Inft.	E	04/25/1864
37	Garland, William J.	13th TN Cav.	B	05/17/1864
38	Green, Athen	13th TN Cav.	C	09/24/1863
39	Green, Samuel	3rd NC Mtd. Inft.	E	03/25/1864
40	Green, Starling P.	13th TN Cav.	C	09/24/1863
41	Green, Thomas	13th TN Cav.	C	09/24/1863
42	Green, Thomas S.	13th TN Cav.	C	09/24/1863
43	Griffin, Isaac	13th TN Cav.	C	03/20/1864
44	Grindstaff, Lawrence E.	3rd NC Mtd. Inft.	E	03/25/1864
45	Guge, Joseph L.	3rd NC Mtd. Inft.	E	03/25/1864
46	Guge, Samuel C.	3rd NC Mtd. Inft.	E	03/25/1864
47	Harreld, Simon	13th TN Cav.	M	05/15/1864
48	Hileman, John C.	3rd NC Mtd. Inft.	E	03/25/1864
49	Hoppes, Joseph H.	13th TN Cav.	C	02/01/1865
50	Howell, Jesse P.	3rd NC Mtd. Inft.	A	10/01/1864
51	Howell, Swinfield	3rd NC Mtd. Inft.	A	10/01/1864
52	Hughes, John	13th TN Cav.	C	09/24/1863
53	Hughes, William J.	6th US Vol. Inft.	H	04/01/1865
54	Huntley, Isaac A.	13th TN Cav.	C	09/24/1863
55	Johnson, Isaac	3rd NC Mtd. Inft.	F	10/26/1864
56	Jones, Thomas M.	13th TN Cav.	C	09/01/1865
57	Kite, Russell	3rd NC Mtd. Inft.	F	10/12/1864
58	Ledford, Thomas	13th TN Cav.	B	12/31/1863
59	Lineback, Henry	13th TN Cav.	C	01/25/1864
60	McGalliard, William H.	3rd NC Mtd. Inft.	A	07/01/1864

61	McGuire, James	3rd NC Mtd. Inft.	F	10/05/1864
62	McKinney, John	13th TN Cav.	C	09/24/1863
63	Oaks, Jeremiah	13th TN Cav.	C	01/31/1864
64	Oaks, Nehemiah	13th TN Cav.	C	09/24/1863
65	Patterson, Calloway	3rd NC Mtd. Inft.	F	10/05/1864
66	Phillips, Guthridge K.	3rd NC Mtd. Inft.	E	03/25/1864
67	Pitman, Reuben	13th TN Cav.	C	09/24/1863
68	Proctor, Reuben	8th TN Cav.	K	08/05/1863
69	Riddle, James M.	3rd NC Mtd. Inft.	E	03/25/1865
70	Scott, Lorenzo D.	13th TN Cav.	H	?
71	Sparks, James	13th TN Cav.	C	09/24/1863
72	Sparks, Lewis M.	3rd NC Mtd. Inft.	A	10/01/1864
73	Sparks, Whitfield	13th TN Cav.	C	10/02/1864
74	Stewart, Joseph S.	3rd NC Mtd. Inft.	F	10/20/1864
75	Stout, Thomas	13th TN Cav.	B	09/23/1863
76	Stout, William	13th TN Cav.	B	05/31/1864
77	Street, Charles	3rd NC Mtd. Inft.	E	03/25/1864
78	Street, John D.	3rd NC Mtd. Inft.	E	05/25/1864
79	Street, Stephen	3rd NC Mtd. Inft.	E	12/03/1864
80	Street, William H.	3rd NC Mtd. Inft.	E	10/14/1864
81	Williams, Thomas	3rd NC Mtd. Inft.	A	08/14/1864
82	Young, Merritt	13th TN Cav.	C	?
83	Young, Strobridge	13th TN Cav.	C	09/24/1863
84	Young, Wilson	13th TN Cav.	C	09/24/1863

POLK COUNTY UNION SOLDIERS

	Name	Regiment	Company	Date of Enlistment
1	Childers, William	US Navy		01/25/1864
2	Ellison, William, Jr.	US Navy		01/25/1864
3	Giles, James M.	?	?	10/15/1864
4	Goings, John	3rd NC Mtd. Inft.	E	04/26/1864
5	Kirkendall, John F.	3rd NC Mtd. Inft.	E	03/25/1864
6	Laughter, Elias	3rd NC Mtd. Inft.	G	11/01/1864
7	Ledbetter, Thomas B.	US Navy		01/09/1865
8	Morrow, G. W.	1st US Vol. Inft.	B	06/14/1864
9	Raines, Nathan	3rd NC Mtd. Inft.	I	03/01/1865
10	Taylor, Obediah	2nd NC Mtd. Inft.	C	01/01/1864
11	Tenison, William P.	1st US Vol. Inft.	B	01/24/1864
12	West, Albert S.	3rd NC Mtd. Inft.	I	03/01/1865

RUTHERFORD COUNTY UNION SOLDIERS

	Name	Regiment	Company	Date of Enlistment
1	Ballard, James E.	3rd NC Mtd. Inft.	A	06/11/1864
2	Ballard, John G.	3rd NC Mtd. Inft.	G	01/31/1865
3	Baynard, Martin	US Navy		12/31/1863
4	Bias, Henry H.	3rd NC Mtd. Inft.	C	09/24/1864
5	Bradley, George W.	2nd NC Mtd. Inft.	B	10/25/1863
6	Bradley, John J.	2nd NC Mtd. Inft.	B	10/01/1863
7	Bradley, William T.	2nd NC Mtd. Inft.	B	09/25/1863
8	Brown, Doctor C.	2nd NC Mtd. Inft.	H	10/01/1863
9	Brown, Fielding	2nd NC Mtd. Inft.	B	09/25/1863
10	Case, William L.	2nd NC Mtd. Inft.	H	10/01/1863
11	Cercy, William	2nd NC Mtd. Inft.	B	09/25/1863
12	Collins, George	2nd NC Mtd. Inft.	H	10/01/1863
13	Collins, Iriah	2nd NC Mtd. Inft.	H	10/01/1863
14	Collins, James T.	2nd NC Mtd. Inft.	H	10/01/1863
15	Cook, Alfred W.	?	?	02/01/1864
16	Dunkin, Alfred J.	2nd NC Mtd. Inft.	H	10/01/1863
17	Foster, Ransom	2nd NC Mtd. Inft.	H	10/01/1863
18	Gibbs, Elias Madison	US Navy		12/31/1863
19	Gibbs, John	2nd NC Mtd. Inft.	H	10/01/1863
20	Gibbs, William	2nd NC Mtd. Inft.	H	10/01/1863
21	Green, George M.	2nd NC Mtd. Inft.	H	11/01/1863
22	Hampton, Daniel	3rd NC Mtd. Inft.	F	03/03/1864
23	Hollifield, Joel A.	3rd NC Mtd. Inft.	A	06/11/1864
24	Jenkins, John	3rd MD Cav.	G	09/05/1863
25	Jones, William	2nd NC Mtd. Inft.	A	04/01/1865
26	Justice, Robert M.	2nd NC Mtd. Inft.	H	10/25/1863
27	Keeter, James C.	5th US Vol. Inft.	H	04/14/1865
28	Kelly, John	2nd NC Mtd. Inft.	F	10/01/1864
29	Marrow, Harrison	2nd NC Mtd. Inft.	D	10/03/1863

30	McMurray, Andrew W.	2nd NC Mtd. Inft.	B	09/25/1863
31	McMurray, William G.	2nd NC Mtd. Inft.	H	12/01/1864
32	Only, Robert H.	2nd NC Mtd. Inft.	B	09/25/1863
33	Parker, Carson	3rd NC Mtd. Inft.	E	03/25/1864
34	Patterson, Luther C.	2nd NC Mtd. Inft.	F	10/01/1863
35	Prather, Amos	2nd NC Mtd. Inft.	D	10/01/1863
36	Rich, William	3rd NC Mtd. Inft.	F	11/11/1864
37	Roach, Newton	1st US Vol. Inft.	D	02/20/1864
38	Robertson, General M.	5th US Vol. Inft.	H	04/14/1865
39	Scroggins, James O.	3rd NC Mtd. Inft.	K	03/01/1865
40	Scroggins, John N.	3rd NC Mtd. Inft.	K	03/01/1865
41	Searcy, Samuel D.	2nd NC Mtd. Inft.	H	10/01/1863
42	Searcy, William B.	3rd US Vol. Inft.	B	10/17/1864
43	Sexton, Elijah	2nd NC Mtd. Inft.	D	10/03/1863
44	Simes, John L.	2nd NC Mtd. Inft.	D	10/01/1863
45	Smith, John	3rd NC Mtd. Inft.	C	01/01/1865
46	Taylor, James M.	2nd NC Mtd. Inft.	A	10/01/1863
47	Turner, Elijah W.	1st US Vol. Inft.	D	02/05/1864
48	Twiggs, John	13th TN Cav.	H	11/09/1863
49	Vess, Zephaniah	2nd NC Mtd. Inft.	B	09/25/1863
50	Walker, Thomas E.	2nd NC Mtd. Inft.	H	12/01/1864
51	Walker, William	3rd NC Mtd. Inft.	I	03/01/1865
52	Wilson, Jesse N.	US Navy		04/14/1865

TRANSYLVANIA COUNTY UNION SOLDIERS

	Name	Regiment	Company	Date of Enlistment
1	Barton, Millington	3rd NC Mtd. Inft.	D	03/02/1864
2	Crook, John P.	3rd NC Mtd. Inft.	E	11/10/1864
3	Garren, Adolphus	3rd NC Mtd. Inft.	E	04/16/1864
4	Henry, Joseph	3rd NC Mtd. Inft.	D	10/12/1864
5	Lanning, Andrew J.	3rd NC Mtd. Inft.	D	03/22/1864
6	Ledbetter, Philo	3rd NC Mtd. Inft.	D	09/05/1864
7	Loftis, Elijah N.	3rd NC Mtd. Inft.	E	12/02/1864
8	Loftis, Frederick F.	3rd NC Mtd. Inft.	E	10/25/1864
9	McCall, Samuel	3rd NC Mtd. Inft.	E	04/16/1864
10	Searcy, David W.	3rd NC Mtd. Inft.	I	10/20/1864
11	Searcy, Elijah J.	3rd NC Mtd. Inft.	I	10/20/1864
12	Simpson, Merritt R.	6th US Vol. Inft.	I	04/02/1865
13	Swangin, Thomas	3rd NC Mtd. Inft.	A	06/11/1864

WATAUGA COUNTY UNION SOLDIERS

	Name	Regiment	Company	Date of Enlistment
1	Barlow, Thomas J.	3rd NC Mtd. Inft.	?	08/07/1864
2	Bowles, Melmoth	13th TN Cav.	M	02/12/1864
3	Bracher, Joseph	3rd NC Mtd. Inft.	H	01/01/1865
4	Campbell, H. H.	1st US Vol. Inft.	F	02/25/1864
5	Cook, John H.	2nd NC Mtd. Inft.	E	04/15/1865
6	Danner, Peter F.	3rd NC Mtd. Inft.	F	09/11/1864
7	Ervin, James M.	3rd NC Mtd. Inft.	C	08/21/1864
8	Ervin, John	3rd NC Mtd. Inft.	C	08/21/1864
9	Farthing, John S.	1st US Vol. Inft.	G	02/26/1864
10	Fletcher, Spencer	3rd TN Mtd. Inft.	A	?
11	Fletcher, Thomas Burt	6th US Vol. Inft.	C	05/05/1865
12	Gragg, John	3rd NC Mtd. Inft.	F	11/01/1864
13	Greene, Levi	2nd NC Mtd. Inft.	E	04/15/1865
14	Harmon, Andrew J.	13th TN Cav.	E	?
15	Hartley, James	3rd NC Mtd. Inft.	B	06/11/1864
16	Hathely, Riley B.	13th TN Cav.	E	09/24/1863
17	Hatley, John F.	13th TN Cav.	E	?
18	Hatley, Wiley	13th TN Cav.	E	?
19	Hilliard, Alfred, Jr.	US Navy		06/10/1864
20	Hodge, Waitsel	13th TN Cav.	C	10/01/1864
21	Hodges, Demarcus	2nd NC Mtd. Inft.	D	04/15/1865
22	Hodges, Willry J.	13th TN Cav.	E	11/08/1863
23	Horton, William R.	3rd NC Mtd. Inft.	I	03/01/1865
24	Hurt, Jesse	3rd NC Mtd. Inft.	A	09/10/1864
25	Isaac, Noah	3rd TN Mtd. Inft.	C	?
26	Isaac, Solomon	US Navy		06/01/1864
27	Keller, Jessie R.	3rd NC Mtd. Inft.	F	07/07/1864
28	Lewis, James	13th TN Cav.	I	09/22/1863

29	Matheson, John	13th TN Cav.	F	09/22/1863
30	McCloud, David F.	3rd NC Mtd. Inft.	F	09/11/1864
31	McGee, James H.	2nd NC Mtd. Inft.	D	10/11/1863
32	Miller, Jesse M.	3rd NC Mtd. Inft.	I	01/01/1865
33	Miller, John	US Navy		01/25/1864
34	Miller, Marcus	3rd NC Mtd. Inft.	I	01/01/1865
35	Moody, Benjamin	13th TN Cav.	A	09/24/1863
36	Moody, Edward C.	2nd NC Mtd. Inft.	B	04/15/1865
37	Rash, Lindsay	3rd NC Mtd. Inft.	A	06/11/1864
38	Reece, John	13th TN Cav.	E	01/01/1865
39	Smith, Francis	3rd NC Mtd. Inft.	B	01/11/1865
40	Spigner, William	3rd NC Mtd. Inft.	I	01/01/1865
41	Strickland, William	1st US Vol. Inft.	F	02/26/1864
42	Thomas, Hezekiah	6th US Vol. Inft.	C	05/05/1865
43	Triplet, Darby	3rd NC Mtd. Inft.	B	08/01/1864
44	Triplet, Moses	3rd NC Mtd. Inft.	B	08/01/1864
45	Tucker, Calvin	3rd NC Mtd. Inft.	F	11/11/1864
46	White, Ambrose	3rd NC Mtd. Inft.	I	01/01/1865
47	Wilson, Marion	13th TN Cav.	E	07/01/1864

WILKES COUNTY UNION SOLDIERS

	Name	*Regiment*	*Company*	*Date of Enlistment*
1	Abshire, Levi	1st US Vol. Inft.	F	06/15/1864
2	Adams, Harper	3rd NC Mtd. Inft.	F	08/06/1864
3	Adams, William H.	3rd NC Mtd. Inft.	H	01/25/1865
4	Bishop, Elbert	13th TN Cav.	I	?
5	Blackburn, Andrew	3rd NC Mtd. Inft.	H	01/25/1865
6	Blackburn, Collumbus F.	3rd NC Mtd. Inft.	C	03/01/1865
7	Blackburn, George F.	3rd NC Mtd. Inft.	H	01/25/1865
8	Blackburn, William	3rd NC Mtd. Inft.	H	01/25/1865
9	Blankenship, John Q.	3rd NC Mtd. Inft.	B	07/02/1864
10	Borders, Drewy	13th TN Cav.	C	09/24/1863
11	Bowers, John F.	3rd NC Mtd. Inft.	I	01/01/1865
12	Bowers, William	3rd NC Mtd. Inft.	I	02/15/1865
13	Brookshire, Noah B.	3rd NC Mtd. Inft.	B	10/06/1864
14	Brown, Aaron	3rd NC Mtd. Inft.	H	01/25/1865
15	Brown, George H.	3rd NC Mtd. Inft.	F	08/06/1864
16	Brown, George W.	2nd US Vol. Inft.	B	01/27/1864
17	Brown, Mark H.	3rd NC Mtd. Inft.	H	01/25/1865
18	Burchett, Martin	1st US Vol. Inft.	B	01/26/1864
19	Burgess, Solomon	3rd NC Mtd. Inft.	H	08/06/1864
20	Burton, William	13th TN Cav.	E	09/21/1863
21	Byrd, William	3rd NC Mtd. Inft.	I	06/01/1865
22	Caudill, Abner	1st US Vol. Inft.	F	02/22/1864
23	Church, Alfred	3rd NC Mtd. Inft.	I	03/08/1865
24	Church, General G. W.	3rd NC Mtd. Inft.	H	01/25/1865
25	Church, Harrison	3rd NC Mtd. Inft.	A	06/11/1864
26	Church, Irvin	Ahl's DE Heavy Artillery		07/27/1863
27	Church, John L.	3rd NC Mtd. Inft.	I	01/01/1865
28	Church, Jordan	3rd NC Mtd. Inft.	H	01/25/1865

29	Church, William F.	US Marine Corps		07/02/1863
30	Clinton, John	3rd NC Mtd. Inft.	H	11/30/1864
31	Cockerham, Joseph	?	?	02/22/1864
32	Cook, Benjamin	3rd NC Mtd. Inft.	F	11/11/1864
33	Darnell, Morgan S.	3rd NC Mtd. Inft.	I	02/15/1865
34	Davis, Nesbet C.	1st US Vol. Inft.	I	06/22/1864
35	Day, Samuel	2nd NC Mtd. Inft.	D	04/15/1865
36	Dowell, Emerald	13th TN Cav.	E	10/28/1863
37	Dowell, James E.	13th TN Cav.	G	10/28/1863
38	Dowell, John L.	13th TN Cav.	G	10/28/1863
39	Edmiston, John	1st US Vol. Inft.	K	06/15/1864
40	Ellis, John E.	2nd NC Mtd. Inft.	C	09/26/1863
41	Griffy, William Thomas	1st CT Cav.	G	10/04/1863
42	Hall, Jesse P.	3rd NC Mtd. Inft.	B	06/17/1864
43	Hall, William H.	1st US Vol. Inft.	F	02/21/1864
44	Handy, Noel	3rd NC Mtd. Inft.	H	01/25/1865
45	Handy, Thomas B.	3rd NC Mtd. Inft.	H	01/25/1865
46	Handy, William H.	1st US Vol. Inft.	K	06/18/1864
47	Hanks, William	13th TN Cav.	E	11/08/1863
48	Hanner, Simpson A.	?	?	01/25/1864
49	Harless, James	1st US Vol. Inft.	H	05/19/1864
50	Harrison, Nathan	13th TN Cav.	E	09/24/1863
51	Hayes, William H.	1st US Vol. Inft.	D	02/10/1864
52	Hays, Joseph F.	3rd NC Mtd. Inft.	F	08/06/1864
53	Heagin, Wilson N.	13th TN Cav.	H	11/01/1863
54	Hendrow, Jesse	3rd NC Mtd. Inft.	F	08/06/1864
55	Howell, Ancy B.	3rd NC Mtd. Inft.	B	10/06/1864
56	Howell, George W.	3rd NC Mtd. Inft.	B	02/15/1865
57	Howell, John O.	3rd NC Mtd. Inft.	B	10/06/1864
58	Humphrey, Young	13th TN Cav.	G	10/22/1863
59	Jennings, Allen	13th TN Cav.	G	10/16/1864

60	Jennings, John J.	3rd NC Mtd. Inft.	H	01/25/1865
61	Jennings, Reuben	3rd NC Mtd. Inft.	F	08/06/1864
62	Johnson, Finley P.	3rd NC Mtd. Inft.	D	08/06/1864
63	Johnson, John	3rd NC Mtd. Inft.	H	02/15/1865
64	Jolley, Milas	13th TN Cav.	A	09/22/1863
65	Jones, Eli	3rd NC Mtd. Inft.	A	06/11/1864
66	Kilby, Samuel	3rd NC Mtd. Inft.	H	01/25/1865
67	Kilby, William J.	3rd NC Mtd. Inft.	H	01/25/1865
68	Lane, Benjamin	13th TN Cav.	H	09/24/1863
69	Laws, Andrew J.	3rd NC Mtd. Inft.	A	06/11/1864
70	Laws, Daniel P.	3rd NC Mtd. Inft.	A	06/11/1864
71	Laws, David	3rd NC Mtd. Inft.	A	06/11/1864
72	Laws, David S.	3rd NC Mtd. Inft.	A	06/11/1864
73	Laws, Rufus	3rd NC Mtd. Inft.	A	06/11/1864
74	Linden, Adolphus	13th TN Cav.	E	02/20/1864
75	Lippord, Lewis	13th TN Cav.	G	09/01/1865
76	Livingston, John	13th TN Cav.	I	01/10/1864
77	Marlow, Harvey	?	?	02/10/1864
78	McCoy, William	13th TN Cav.	E	10/01/1864
79	McGlammon, ?	3rd NC Mtd. Inft.	A	06/11/1864
80	McGlumley, ?	3rd NC Mtd. Inft.	A	06/11/1864
81	Miller, Columbus	3rd NC Mtd. Inft.	A	06/11/1864
82	Minton, Pervis	3rd NC Mtd. Inft.	A	06/11/1864
83	Moore, Riley L.	1st US Vol. Inft.	G	02/10/1864
84	Nichols, Abraham	3rd NC Mtd. Inft.	F	08/06/1864
85	Nichols, Henry H.	3rd NC Mtd. Inft.	F	08/06/1864
86	Nicholson, Lazarus	?	?	05/18/1864
87	Norman, Joseph T.	3rd NC Mtd. Inft.	I	01/01/1865
88	Norris, Jesse F.	1st US Vol. Inft.	G	05/27/1864
89	Pardew, Abner	13th TN Cav.	E	09/24/1863
90	Pardue, Joel	13th TN Cav.	G	07/29/1865

91	Payne, Zebulon	13th TN Cav.	E	09/24/1863
92	Perdue, Joseph H.	3rd NC Mtd. Inft.	I	03/06/1865
93	Phillips, Hugh	3rd NC Mtd. Inft.	H	01/25/1865
94	Porter, James M.	3rd NC Mtd. Inft.	D	08/06/1864
95	Porter, William F.	3rd NC Mtd. Inft.	D	08/06/1864
96	Price, Isaiah	3rd NC Mtd. Inft.	G	09/01/1864
97	Queen, Finley A.	3rd NC Mtd. Inft.	I	01/01/1865
98	Queen, Pickney H.	3rd NC Mtd. Inft.	I	01/01/1865
99	Queen, Samuel R.	3rd NC Mtd. Inft.	I	01/01/1865
100	Queen, William R.	3rd NC Mtd. Inft.	I	01/01/1865
101	Rash, Thomas J.	13th TN Cav.	I	03/01/1864
102	Reece, Hugh	13th TN Cav.	I	09/13/1864
103	Rhoads, John A.	3rd NC Mtd. Inft.	H	01/25/1865
104	Rhoads, William D.	3rd NC Mtd. Inft.	H	01/25/1865
105	Rhodes, Benjamin	3rd NC Mtd. Inft.	H	11/01/1864
106	Richardson, Moses F.	3rd NC Mtd. Inft.	H	01/25/1865
107	Rotan, John	13th TN Cav.	E	09/24/1863
108	Russell, John P.	3rd NC Mtd. Inft.	B	10/27/1864
109	Russell, Noah	3rd NC Mtd. Inft.	A	06/11/1864
110	Sanders, David	3rd MD Cav.	E	09/22/1863
111	Sebastine, Lewis W.	3rd NC Mtd. Inft.	F	02/16/1865
112	Shores, James C.	4th US Vol. Inft.	B	10/12/1864
113	Shumate, Enoch C.	3rd NC Mtd. Inft.	H	01/25/1865
114	Shumate, Mark H.	3rd NC Mtd. Inft.	H	01/25/1865
115	Shumate, Wesley	3rd NC Mtd. Inft.	H	01/25/1865
116	Simmons, Henry C.	2nd NC Mtd. Inft.	E	04/15/1865
117	Sparks, Elijah	13th TN Cav.	D	04/18/1864
118	Sprinkle, Obadiah	US Navy		05/23/1864
119	Triplet, Elbert G.	3rd NC Mtd. Inft.	H	10/01/1864
120	Triplet, Thomas H.	2nd NC Mtd. Inft.	D	11/10/1863
121	Triplett, Elbert	1st US Vol. Inft.	B	01/26/1864

122	Triplett, Sidney	US Marine Corps		07/04/1863
123	Triplett, Thomas	13th TN Cav.	E	09/24/1863
124	Triplett, William	US Marine Corps		12/02/1863
125	Tyre, Thomas M.	13th TN Cav.	I	09/22/1863
126	Voncannon, Abram B.	?	?	02/10/1864
127	Walker, James	3rd NC Mtd. Inft.	G	10/01/1864
128	Walker, James W.	3rd NC Mtd. Inft.	H	02/16/1865
129	Walker, John A.	3rd NC Mtd. Inft.	H	01/25/1865
130	Walker, Robert	3rd NC Mtd. Inft.	H	02/15/1865
131	Walkins, John W.	US Navy		01/25/1864
132	Wallace, Samuel	3rd NC Mtd. Inft.	I	01/01/1865
133	Watkins, Andrew	13th TN Cav.	H	12/14/1863
134	Watson, Melton	1st US Vol. Inft.	B	01/24/1864
135	Watson, William	13th TN Cav.	E	09/24/1863
136	Wilborn, James M.	3rd NC Mtd. Inft.	I	01/01/1865
137	Wood, William M.	3rd NC Mtd. Inft.	H	01/25/1865
138	Wyatt, Victory	1st US Vol. Inft.	F	01/25/1864
139	Yates, Alfred	1st US Vol. Inft.	H	05/22/1864
140	Yeates, Jesse F.	3rd NC Mtd. Inft.	H	12/27/1864
141	Yeates, John D.	3rd NC Mtd. Inft.	H	12/27/1864
142	Yelton, James	2nd NC Mtd. Inft.	A	09/15/1863
143	Younce, George	13th TN Cav.	G	10/01/1864
144	Younger, Joseph	3rd NC Mtd. Inft.	I	01/01/1864
145	Younger, William G.	3rd NC Mtd. Inft.	F	08/06/1864

YANCEY COUNTY UNION SOLDIERS

	Name	Regiment	Company	Date of Enlistment
1	Allen, Adacrum	3rd NC Mtd. Inft.	K	03/01/1865
2	Allen, Andrew J.	3rd NC Mtd. Inft.	A	10/01/1864
3	Allen, Ervin	3rd NC Mtd. Inft.	A	08/01/1864
4	Allen, George	3rd NC Mtd. Inft.	A	08/01/1864
5	Allen, Nathaniel	3rd NC Mtd. Inft.	J	12/01/1864
6	Allen, Young	3rd NC Mtd. Inft.	K	03/01/1865
7	Anders, David H.	3rd NC Mtd. Inft.	K	03/01/1865
8	Anders, James B.	3rd NC Mtd. Inft.	K	03/01/1865
9	Anders, Jasper E.	3rd NC Mtd. Inft.	K	03/01/1865
10	Anders, William F.	3rd NC Mtd. Inft.	K	03/01/1865
11	Austin, Andrew T.	3rd NC Mtd. Inft.	K	03/01/1865
12	Austin, Clingman L.	3rd NC Mtd. Inft.	K	03/01/1865
13	Austin, Edward K.	3rd NC Mtd. Inft.	K	03/01/1865
14	Austin, William A.	3rd NC Mtd. Inft.	G	10/10/1864
15	Bailey, Calvin	13th TN Cav.	M	05/15/1864
16	Bailey, Dobson	13th TN Cav.	M	05/15/1864
17	Bailey, Jefferson	3rd NC Mtd. Inft.	F	08/04/1864
18	Ballard, John K.	3rd NC Mtd. Inft.	C	09/24/1864
19	Ballew, Marion	3rd NC Mtd. Inft.	A	06/11/1864
20	Banks, Andrew J.	2nd NC Mtd. Inft.	E	09/01/1863
21	Banks, Berry P.	3rd NC Mtd. Inft.	K	03/01/1865
22	Banks, Edward	3rd NC Mtd. Inft.	K	03/01/1865
23	Banks, Ezekial	3rd NC Mtd. Inft.	A	06/11/1864
24	Banks, Samuel B.	3rd NC Mtd. Inft.	K	03/01/1865
25	Banks, William B.	3rd NC Mtd. Inft.	K	03/01/1865
26	Barnett, Simon	13th TN Cav.	B	02/24/1864
27	Bennett, Abraham	3rd NC Mtd. Inft.	A	06/11/1864
28	Bennett, Archibald	3rd NC Mtd. Inft.	A	06/11/1864
29	Bennett, Baxter	3rd NC Mtd. Inft.	A	06/11/1864

30	Bennett, Jeremiah	3rd NC Mtd. Inft.	F	07/01/1864
31	Bennett, John	3rd NC Mtd. Inft.	A	06/11/1864
32	Bennett, John Jr.	3rd NC Mtd. Inft.	A	06/11/1864
33	Bennett, William	3rd NC Mtd. Inft.	A	06/11/1864
34	Boon, Amos	3rd NC Mtd. Inft.	K	03/01/1865
35	Bradford, Ervin	3rd NC Mtd. Inft.	E	03/25/1864
36	Bradford, John	3rd NC Mtd. Inft.	E	03/25/1864
37	Briggs, Allison	2nd NC Mtd. Inft.	A	10/25/1863
38	Briggs, Jasper	2nd NC Mtd. Inft.	A	10/25/1863
39	Bryant, Allen M.	13th TN Cav.	M	09/23/1863
40	Bryant, James	3rd NC Mtd. Inft.	A	04/01/1864
41	Bryant, Nathan	13th TN Cav.	M	09/23/1863
42	Bryant, Thomas	3rd NC Mtd. Inft.	A	04/13/1864
43	Buckner, Levi	3rd NC Mtd. Inft.	K	03/01/1865
44	Bullman, John	2nd NC Mtd. Inft.	A	09/15/1863
45	Burleson, James	3rd NC Mtd. Inft.	G	10/01/1864
46	Burrison, John W.	2nd NC Mtd. Inft.	H	10/01/1863
47	Byrd, George	3rd NC Mtd. Inft.	E	03/25/1864
48	Byrd, Lace	13th TN Cav.	B	09/23/1863
49	Byrd, Mitchell	3rd NC Mtd. Inft.	E	07/25/1864
50	Byrd, Samuel	3rd NC Mtd. Inft.	I	03/02/1865
51	Callaway, Thomas	2nd NC Mtd. Inft.	H	10/01/1863
52	Chandler, John	2nd NC Mtd. Inft.	E	08/09/1864
53	Chapel, James W.	3rd NC Mtd. Inft.	F	11/11/1864
54	Clark, Silas J.	3rd NC Mtd. Inft.	A	06/11/1864
55	Clemens, John	2nd NC Mtd. Inft.	A	09/15/1863
56	Clinton, James	13th TN Cav.	B	07/15/1864
57	Cooper, Joel W.	3rd NC Mtd. Inft.	A	06/11/1864
58	Cooper, John G.	3rd NC Mtd. Inft.	F	04/05/1864
59	Cooper, William A.	3rd NC Mtd. Inft.	F	06/11/1864
60	Cordell, James H.	3rd NC Mtd. Inft.	C	06/30/1864

61	Cranford, Henry	3rd NC Mtd. Inft.	K	03/01/1865
62	Davis, Jacob	3rd NC Mtd. Inft.	E	03/25/1864
63	Davis, Stephen M.	2nd NC Mtd. Inft.	A	09/15/1863
64	Doby, George F.	3rd NC Mtd. Inft.	K	03/01/1865
65	Downin, Samuel	3rd NC Mtd. Inft.	D	04/26/1864
66	Edwards, George	13th TN Cav.	B	09/23/1864
67	Edwards, John	3rd NC Mtd. Inft.	E	09/01/1864
68	Edwards, Robert	3rd NC Mtd. Inft.	E	09/01/1864
69	Edwards, Thomas S.	3rd NC Mtd. Inft.	G	02/01/1865
70	Edwards, William	3rd NC Mtd. Inft.	G	02/01/1865
71	Fender, Allen	3rd NC Mtd. Inft.	G	10/01/1864
72	Fender, Wiley	3rd NC Mtd. Inft.	G	10/01/1864
73	Fender, William	3rd NC Mtd. Inft.	G	10/01/1864
74	Forbes, Rickler	3rd NC Mtd. Inft.	E	03/25/1864
75	Forbes, William	3rd NC Mtd. Inft.	E	03/25/1864
76	Franklin, Andrew J.	2nd NC Mtd. Inft.	E	09/01/1863
77	Franklin, Francis M.	2nd NC Mtd. Inft.	E	09/01/1863
78	Franklin, George	2nd NC Mtd. Inft.	E	09/01/1863
79	Franklin, John	2nd NC Mtd. Inft.	E	10/01/1863
80	Frazier, David C.	13th TN Cav.	B	09/23/1864
81	Gardner, Thomas J.	3rd NC Mtd. Inft.	K	03/01/1865
82	Garland, John C.	3rd NC Mtd. Inft.	F	07/02/1864
83	Garland, John M.	13th TN Cav.	B	05/17/1864
84	Garland, Reuben	3rd NC Mtd. Inft.	F	06/07/1864
85	Garland, Zachariah	13th TN Cav.	B	05/31/1864
86	Garner, William	3rd NC Mtd. Inft.	G	10/21/1864
87	Gentry, George	2nd NC Mtd. Inft.	C	09/26/1863
88	Gentry, Hiram	3rd NC Mtd. Inft.	C	09/12/1864
89	Gentry, William	2nd NC Mtd. Inft.	E	09/01/1863
90	Gillespie, Fry B.	13th TN Cav.	G	09/24/1863
91	Gosnell, Simeon	2nd NC Mtd. Inft.	E	09/01/1863

92	Grogan, Jordan	4th TN Inft.	G	?
93	Hamlet, Oliver Merritt	4th TN Inft.	H	?
94	Hampton, Christopher C.	3rd NC Mtd. Inft.	D	11/10/1864
95	Hampton, Henry M.	3rd NC Mtd. Inft.	I	03/02/1865
96	Hampton, William F.	US Navy		02/05/1864
97	Hansley, A. J.	3rd NC Mtd. Inft.	C	08/21/1864
98	Harrison, Joseph W.	13th TN Cav.	E	?
99	Hatton, Warren A.	13th TN Cav.	E	?
100	Headrick, James	3rd NC Mtd. Inft.	H	01/20/1865
101	Hensley, Abraham	3rd NC Mtd. Inft.	A	10/01/1864
102	Hensley, Adolphus	3rd NC Mtd. Inft.	K	03/01/1865
103	Hensley, Beverly	2nd NC Mtd. Inft.	E	09/01/1863
104	Hensley, Ephraim	2nd NC Mtd. Inft.	E	09/01/1863
105	Hensley, Ezekial	3rd NC Mtd. Inft.	D	08/12/1864
106	Hensley, George W.	2nd NC Mtd. Inft.	E	09/01/1863
107	Hensley, Goodson M.	3rd NC Mtd. Inft.	K	03/01/1865
108	Hensley, James W.	13th TN Cav.	K	01/26/1864
109	Hensley, Jesse	6th US Vol. Inft.	D	03/24/1865
110	Hensley, John H.	3rd NC Mtd. Inft.	G	08/10/1864
111	Hensley, Klingman	3rd NC Mtd. Inft.	C	11/05/1864
112	Hensley, Logan	13th TN Cav.	K	01/26/1864
113	Hensley, Lorenzo	3rd NC Mtd. Inft.	C	11/05/1864
114	Hensley, Silas B.	3rd NC Mtd. Inft.	K	03/01/1865
115	Hensley, William	13th TN Cav.	K	01/26/1864
116	Hensley, William	2nd NC Mtd. Inft.	E	09/01/1863
117	Hensley, William	3rd NC Mtd. Inft.	K	03/01/1865
118	Hensley, William M.	6th US Vol. Inft.	?	03/25/1865
119	Hensley, Wilson	3rd NC Mtd. Inft.	G	10/14/1864
120	Hensly, Howell	3rd NC Mtd. Inft.	E	09/01/1864
121	Hensly, Thomas	3rd NC Mtd. Inft.	G	10/01/1864

122	Higgins, Gaston	3rd NC Mtd. Inft.	G	10/01/1864
123	Higgins, James Erwin	2nd US Vol. Inft.	I	10/13/1864
124	Higgins, James K.	3rd NC Mtd. Inft.	G	10/01/1864
125	Higgins, John	3rd NC Mtd. Inft.	A	06/11/1864
126	Higgins, Lucius	3rd NC Mtd. Inft.	G	02/01/1865
127	Higgins, William M.	3rd NC Mtd. Inft.	E	10/26/1864
128	Honeycutt, David	13th TN Cav.	B	09/23/1863
129	Honeycutt, Lafayette	13th TN Cav.	M	05/15/1864
130	Honeycutt, Noah	3rd NC Mtd. Inft.	E	09/01/1864
131	Honeycutt, Rubin	3rd NC Mtd. Inft.	F	06/04/1864
132	Hoover, Daniel	3rd NC Mtd. Inft.	A	12/01/1864
133	Howell, James	3rd NC Mtd. Inft.	F	07/01/1864
134	Hughes, James	3rd NC Mtd. Inft.	F	02/16/1865
135	Jarrett, Eli H.	3rd NC Mtd. Inft.	C	06/11/1864
136	Johnson, George	3rd NC Mtd. Inft.	G	10/01/1864
137	Keller, Nicholas	3rd NC Mtd. Inft.	F	07/01/1864
138	Killian, John C.	3rd NC Mtd. Inft.	D	06/30/1864
139	Landers, Beverly	2nd NC Mtd. Inft.	E	09/01/1863
140	Landers, Tilman H.	2nd NC Mtd. Inft.	E	09/01/1863
141	Laws, James B.	3rd NC Mtd. Inft.	A	06/11/1864
142	Laws, James W.	3rd NC Mtd. Inft.	A	06/11/1864
143	Laws, John M.	3rd NC Mtd. Inft.	I	01/01/1865
144	Ledford, James H.	US Navy		06/01/1864
145	Lewis, James W.	3rd NC Mtd. Inft.	G	10/18/1864
146	Lewis, Matthew A.	3rd NC Mtd. Inft.	K	03/01/1865
147	Mace, Solomon	2nd NC Mtd. Inft.	F	10/01/1863
148	Masters, Abraham	3rd NC Mtd. Inft.	F	06/01/1864
149	McClean, Sidney	3rd NC Mtd. Inft.	G	05/20/1864
150	McCourry, Oliver	1st US Vol. Inft.	B	06/14/1864
151	McCoury, James	3rd NC Mtd. Inft.	K	03/01/1865
152	McCoury, James O.	3rd NC Mtd. Inft.	K	03/01/1865

153	McCoury, Tilman H.	3rd NC Mtd. Inft.	K	03/01/1865
154	McCoury, Zephaniah	3rd NC Mtd. Inft.	K	03/01/1865
155	McCoy, Peter	2nd NC Mtd. Inft.	E	09/01/1863
156	McCracken, John	3rd NC Mtd. Inft.	G	02/01/1865
157	McDowell, Charles L.	2nd NC Mtd. Inft.	A	09/15/1863
158	McDowell, George M.	2nd NC Mtd. Inft.	B	09/25/1863
159	McIntosh, John	2nd NC Mtd. Inft.	E	04/08/1864
160	McIntosh, John	3rd NC Mtd. Inft.	B	07/03/1864
161	McInturff, Clayton	13th TN Cav.	L	01/10/1864
162	McKinney, Samuel	3rd NC Mtd. Inft.	I	03/02/1865
163	McMahan, Charles B.	2nd NC Mtd. Inft.	H	01/20/1865
164	McMahan, David A.	2nd NC Mtd. Inft.	H	10/01/1863
165	McMahan, Edward	2nd NC Mtd. Inft.	H	10/01/1863
166	McMahan, John Y.	2nd NC Mtd. Inft.	H	10/01/1863
167	McMahon, Archibald B.	3rd NC Mtd. Inft.	K	03/01/1865
168	McMahon, George	3rd NC Mtd. Inft.	K	03/01/1865
169	McMahon, James	3rd NC Mtd. Inft.	K	03/01/1865
170	McMahon, William B.	3rd NC Mtd. Inft.	A	07/01/1864
171	McNeal, Alexander	3rd NC Mtd. Inft.	A	10/01/1864
172	McNeal, Archibald	3rd NC Mtd. Inft.	A	10/01/1864
173	McNeal, John	3rd NC Mtd. Inft.	A	10/01/1864
174	McPeters, Jonathan	3rd NC Mtd. Inft.	I	03/01/1865
175	Medcalf, John	3rd NC Mtd. Inft.	G	08/01/1864
176	Miller, Hiram	3rd NC Mtd. Inft.	A	06/11/1864
177	Miller, Jacob	3rd NC Mtd. Inft.	A	04/01/1864
178	Miller, John	3rd NC Mtd. Inft.	A	03/10/1864
179	Miller, Samuel	US Navy		06/10/1864
180	Miller, Timothy	3rd NC Mtd. Inft.	F	07/07/1864
181	Morrison, James	3rd NC Mtd. Inft.	K	03/01/1865
182	Moss, William	3rd NC Mtd. Inft.	K	03/01/1865
183	Norton, Balis	2nd NC Mtd. Inft.	E	09/01/1863

184	Norton, David	2nd NC Mtd. Inft.	E	09/01/1863
185	Norton, Jesse	2nd NC Mtd. Inft.	E	09/01/1863
186	Norton, Martin	2nd NC Mtd. Inft.	E	09/01/1863
187	Norton, Roderick	2nd NC Mtd. Inft.	E	09/01/1863
188	Norton, William	2nd NC Mtd. Inft.	E	09/01/1863
189	Ogle, William B.	3rd NC Mtd. Inft.	G	10/01/1864
190	Penland, Charles A.	3rd NC Mtd. Inft.	G	10/01/1864
191	Penland, Jesse	3rd NC Mtd. Inft.	G	10/01/1864
192	Petersen, Lawson	3rd NC Mtd. Inft.	A	06/11/1864
193	Petersen, Moses	3rd NC Mtd. Inft.	A	06/11/1864
194	Petersen, Moses Jr.	3rd NC Mtd. Inft.	A	06/11/1864
195	Petersen, Ruben	3rd NC Mtd. Inft.	A	06/11/1864
196	Petersen, Samuel	3rd NC Mtd. Inft.	A	06/11/1864
197	Phillips, William	3rd NC Mtd. Inft.	E	03/01/1865
198	Phillips, William J.	3rd NC Mtd. Inft.	E	09/01/1864
199	Phipps, Jacob N.	3rd NC Mtd. Inft.	K	03/01/1865
200	Radford, Samuel F.	3rd NC Mtd. Inft.	K	03/15/1865
201	Ramsey, John	2nd NC Mtd. Inft.	C	09/26/1863
202	Ramsey, Joseph R.	3rd NC Mtd. Inft.	A	06/11/1864
203	Rathbone, Henry C.	2nd NC Mtd. Inft.	H	10/01/1863
204	Ray, Albert	7th US Cav.	?	09/01/1863
205	Ray, Barnett	3rd NC Mtd. Inft.	K	03/01/1865
206	Ray, Hiram	3rd NC Mtd. Inft.	I	03/01/1865
207	Ray, James A.	3rd NC Mtd. Inft.	A	11/02/1864
208	Ray, James M.	3rd NC Mtd. Inft.	E	03/01/1865
209	Ray, John H.	3rd NC Mtd. Inft.	K	03/14/1865
210	Ray, Leander	3rd NC Mtd. Inft.	K	03/01/1865
211	Ray, Nathan M.	3rd NC Mtd. Inft.	K	03/01/1865
212	Ray, Samuel B.	3rd NC Mtd. Inft.	K	03/01/1865
213	Ray, Samuel P.	2nd NC Mtd. Inft.	H	10/01/1863
214	Ray, Thomas E.	3rd NC Mtd. Inft.	K	03/01/1865

215	Ray, William H.	3rd NC Mtd. Inft.	K	03/01/1865
216	Renfrow, Thomas	3rd NC Mtd. Inft.	D	07/07/1864
217	Rice, Albert	3rd NC Mtd. Inft.	K	03/01/1865
218	Rice, Hiram	2nd NC Mtd. Inft.	C	09/26/1863
219	Rice, Stephen	2nd NC Mtd. Inft.	A	09/15/1863
220	Rice, Thomas J.	2nd NC Mtd. Inft.	C	03/01/1864
221	Riddle, Hiram B.	2nd NC Mtd. Inft.	C	10/01/1863
222	Riddle, James E.	2nd NC Mtd. Inft.	C	10/01/1863
223	Riddle, John	3rd NC Mtd. Inft.	E	07/25/1864
224	Riddle, Marvill	3rd NC Mtd. Inft.	K	03/01/1865
225	Riddle, Nathan	3rd NC Mtd. Inft.	E	03/25/1865
226	Riddle, William M.	3rd NC Mtd. Inft.	K	03/01/1865
227	Roberson, Young	3rd NC Mtd. Inft.	K	03/01/1865
228	Robertson, Greenberry	2nd NC Mtd. Inft.	B	09/25/1863
229	Roland, George W.	1st US Vol. Inft.	B	01/24/1864
230	Sams, Ezekial	2nd NC Mtd. Inft.	E	09/01/1863
231	Sams, Robert B.	3rd NC Mtd. Inft.	B	07/02/1864
232	Shelton, David Jr.	2nd NC Mtd. Inft.	E	09/01/1863
233	Shelton, David Sr.	2nd NC Mtd. Inft.	E	09/01/1863
234	Shelton, George	2nd NC Mtd. Inft.	E	09/01/1863
235	Shelton, John	2nd NC Mtd. Inft.	E	09/01/1863
236	Shelton, William	2nd NC Mtd. Inft.	E	09/01/1863
237	Sheppard, John W.	3rd NC Mtd. Inft.	K	03/01/1865
238	Sheppard, Mitchell G.	3rd NC Mtd. Inft.	K	03/01/1865
239	Sheppard, Thomas E.	3rd NC Mtd. Inft.	K	03/01/1865
240	Shinolt, Calvin	3rd NC Mtd. Inft.	B	06/25/1864
241	Sparks, Ervin	3rd NC Mtd. Inft.	K	03/01/1865
242	Stanton, John	2nd NC Mtd. Inft.	E	09/01/1863
243	Sylvers, James	3rd NC Mtd. Inft.	A	03/01/1865
244	Taylor, John W.	3rd NC Mtd. Inft.	E	09/01/1864
245	Thomas, David	2nd NC Mtd. Inft.	C	03/01/1864

246	Thompson, James M.	2nd NC Mtd. Inft.	A	09/15/1863
247	Thompson, Joseph	2nd NC Mtd. Inft.	A	09/15/1863
248	Tipton, Alfred D.	3rd NC Mtd. Inft.	B	06/13/1864
249	Tipton, Charles	3rd NC Mtd. Inft.	A	06/25/1864
250	Tipton, David P.	3rd NC Mtd. Inft.	A	06/11/1864
251	Tipton, John D.	3rd NC Mtd. Inft.	A	06/11/1864
252	Tipton, Jonathan	3rd NC Mtd. Inft.	A	06/11/1864
253	Tipton, Samuel	3rd NC Mtd. Inft.	F	10/14/1864
254	Tipton, Sanders H.	3rd NC Mtd. Inft.	G	10/01/1864
255	Tipton, Sebron	US Navy		10/02/1863
256	Tipton, Valentine	3rd NC Mtd. Inft.	G	10/01/1864
257	Tipton, Wiley	13th TN Cav.	B	02/24/1864
258	Tipton, William	3rd NC Mtd. Inft.	F	07/07/1864
259	Tompkins, Steven	3rd NC Mtd. Inft.	B	06/22/1864
260	Webb, Joseph M.	3rd NC Mtd. Inft.	F	10/05/1864
261	Welch, Bennett H.	3rd NC Mtd. Inft.	K	03/17/1865
262	Welch, Sydney	3rd NC Mtd. Inft.	K	03/17/1865
263	Wheeler, Hiram N.	2nd NC Mtd. Inft.	H	10/01/1863
264	Wheeler, James M.	2nd NC Mtd. Inft.	H	06/20/1864
265	Wheeler, John H.	3rd NC Mtd. Inft.	C	09/06/1864
266	Whitson, Isaac	3rd NC Mtd. Inft.	D	07/07/1864
267	Whitson, Madison	3rd NC Mtd. Inft.	G	02/01/1865
268	Williams, Silas	3rd NC Mtd. Inft.	H	02/01/1865
269	Williams, William	3rd NC Mtd. Inft.	F	10/01/1864
270	Willis, John A.	3rd NC Mtd. Inft.	H	10/01/1864
271	Wilson, Edward	3rd NC Mtd. Inft.	H	01/31/1865
272	Wilson, James M.	1st US Vol. Inft.	B	06/14/1864
273	Wilson, John	3rd NC Mtd. Inft.	K	03/01/1865
274	Wilson, John C.	3rd NC Mtd. Inft.	E	08/12/1864
275	Wilson, Levi	3rd NC Mtd. Inft.	F	08/01/1864
276	Wilson, Thomas J.	3rd NC Mtd. Inft.	K	03/01/1865

277	Wilson, William	3rd NC Mtd. Inft.	E	09/01/1864
278	Wilson, William B.	3rd NC Mtd. Inft.	B	08/22/1864
279	Worley, Wiley G.	3rd NC Mtd. Inft.	E	03/25/1864
280	Young, Alford	13th TN Cav.	M	08/01/1864
281	Young, James W.	3rd NC Mtd. Inft.	G	10/15/1864

Chapter Four

—— CONFEDERATE TROOPS FROM WESTERN NORTH CAROLINA ——
TOTAL ESTIMATE: 26,000

"How many Confederate troops served from western North Carolina?"

In researching this question I checked some available sources that were used for previous estimates. It seems that most of these counts or estimates were between nineteen and twenty thousand. At least two well-known historians have published estimates of twenty thousand. I inquired as to what sources were used to count these troops and discovered that they had not counted them. They had used counts previously established by earlier historians. That seemed perfectly reasonable to me so I adopted the number and used it accordingly. My desire to go directly to the sources and count them myself was still unsatisfied.

As time went on and I continued my research I became increasingly concerned that previous counts might not have been accurate. It also appeared to me that biased historians used different methodology to count Confederate or Union troops. In some cases the inaccurate counts were purely accidental. A researcher might use one historian's estimate of Union troops and another historian's estimate of Confederate troops. The problems with that approach are many, but the most striking and obvious one is that the Confederate estimate might be from thirty counties and the Union estimate from ten or vice versa.

Beginning in late 2000 I began to count them myself, one at a time. It should be noted that previous estimates or counts were hampered by a significant disadvantage: some troop records are still incomplete. *North Carolina Troops, 1861-1865,* published by the North Carolina Office of Archives and History, is still a work in progress. As of May 2006 those records only go up to the 68th Regiment. There were more than eighty regiments. To complete a reasonable estimate one is required to find other sources. I made no attempt to include the Militia, Home Guard, The Invalid Corps, Junior Reserves, or Senior Reserves in my count. Such inclusion would add thousands to the Confederate count.

COUNT METHODOLOGY

For the purpose of evaluating the following count/estimate of Confederate troops and casualties the reader should consider several factors.

It is reasonable to assume that an exact count is impossible but one can come very close. I used two primary sources for my count: *North Carolina Troops, 1861-1865,* and *Moore's Roster of North Carolina Troops. Moore's Roster* was used to count troops past the 68th Regiment.[1] It does not contain as much information as *North Carolina Troops* does but it is useful nonetheless. Casualty information is not available in *Moore's Roster.*

The count included in this book is a raw count of names on troop rosters of companies formed in any given western county. In some cases a name can be found listed with a western North Carolina company that may appear to be a man from a county outside the area. That issue was carefully considered by the author and determined to be a "wash." A soldier serving with a western North Carolina company whose home was outside the area is offset by the probability that a soldier from the area served in a company formed outside of western North Carolina, balancing out the estimate.

Regimental officers and staff were not counted because in most cases these men also appear at the company level. The 65th North Carolina Infantry Regiment was not counted at all because it appears to be made up exclusively of transfers. Excluding them prevents some possible duplication.

The largest margin of error comes from duplications that occur when one man's name appears in the record more than once as a result of transfer or promotion. In some companies there is very little repetition, but in others the numbers are considerable. When giving a final estimate or total count of names on Confederate rosters an adjustment has been made. The Confederate estimate has been reduced by 1,282 names to offset possible repetition. The result is a final estimate of 26,000 men from western North Carolina in the Confederate army at some time during the war.

Since rosters of these men are already available I will make no attempt to list them by name in this work. Instead I have read and analyzed each of the 27,000 records where possible for casualty information. Since *North Carolina Troops, 1861-1865* is completed only up through the 68th North Carolina Infantry Regiment I was limited on how far the count could go. Using *North Carolina Troops* as a primary source I have counted those killed in battle, wounds reported, captured, died of noncombat causes, and died in Union prisons.

In cases where "killed in battle" is used or applied it refers to men who were either killed in battle or said to have "died of wounds." In some cases the author determined a soldier to have been killed in battle by the timing of death even if the record did not specifically state "died of wounds." For example a soldier might be listed as wounded at the battle of Gettysburg, then listed as having died on August 2, 1863. Based on the severity of the wound or other information that soldier might be counted as "killed in battle."

In the case of wounds reported it gets more complicated. The reader might incorrectly assume that because company A had fifty wounds reported, that fifty men were wounded. There may have been only forty men wounded but ten men were wounded twice. There are numerous cases of men being wounded two, three, even four or five times. Each wound is counted separately. Several dozen men had a finger, thumb, hand, or fingers amputated and yet they were still returned to duty.

When it comes to captures the same circumstances apply. There are many examples of men who were captured, then exchanged, then captured again. There are examples of men being captured as many as three times. Therefore, one man might account for several wounds, two captures, and also killed in battle.

The category of noncombat deaths includes mostly men who died of disease. There were several thousand of those. It also includes a few examples of accidental deaths. Apparently, train accidents were a significant danger to Confederate troops. Upon reading the records one realizes that the cry of approaching enemy soldiers must have been most feared, but the onset of dysentery was more likely to kill soldiers than enemy fire.

Perhaps the most shocking discovery involving my research is the number of local men who died in Union prisons. Also included in this figure are a handful of men who died in Union custody while being transported as prisoners of war. There are one or two examples of men who died on the exchange boat headed for the South.

It has been documented that Union prisons were in some cases "worse than Andersonville," the notorious Confederate prison in Georgia. In Union prisons Confederates were often the victims of "torture," "murder," and purposeful starvation.[2]

Early Confederate loyalty of mountain men is well documented by their volunteer service. By fall 1861 one in fifteen of the entire mountain population had volunteered to fight for the Confederate cause, compared to only one in nineteen for the rest of the state.[3] When conscription was implemented in April 1862 thousands more volunteered rather than be conscripted.

REFERENCES
1. Moore, John W., *Roster of North Carolina Troops in the War Between the States*, Ashe and Gatlin, Raleigh, North Carolina, 1882.
2. *Eighty Acres of Hell,* The History Channel, A&E Television Networks, 2002.
3. Cotton, William D., *Appalachian North Carolina: A Political Study, 1860-1889,* University of North Carolina, 1954, page 125.

"As they walked through Fort Gregg and the surrounding Petersburg trenches following the Confederate evacuation on April 2, [1865] the victorious Federals could not fail to notice the beardless faces or the silver strands of hair of many of the fallen Southerners. Major Washington Roebling wrote: 'Old men with silver locks lay dead, side by side with mere boys of thirteen or fourteen. It almost makes one sorry to have to fight against a people who show such devotion for their homes and their country.'"

Civil War Times, Vol. XLIV, No. 6, January 2006

CONFEDERATE SERVICE TOTALS—WESTERN NORTH CAROLINA 1861-1865

County	Total Men In Service	Total Wounds	Captured	Killed in Battle	Non-Combat Deaths	Died in Union Prisons	Total Deaths
Ashe	1224	268	277	107	141	34	282
Buncombe	2746	410	432	145	309	70	524
Burke	1450	293	395	106	163	39	308
Caldwell	1272	353	299	121	135	49	305
Catawba	1547	534	623	204	227	69	500
Cherokee	953	89	128	33	79	21	133
Clay	454	89	66	17	29	23	69
Cleveland	2052	587	640	281	324	83	688
Haywood	1504	126	279	39	105	78	222
Henderson	1296	209	277	81	129	63	273
Jackson	1184	114	216	39	61	49	149
Macon	1267	157	240	51	111	39	201
Madison	1969	120	503	34	134	78	246
McDowell	1018	244	261	99	154	36	289
Mitchell	771	94	55	23	59	5	87
Polk	465	67	120	26	81	15	122
Rutherford	1981	298	443	121	263	74	458
Transylvania	549	56	159	15	36	40	91
Watauga	936	199	206	75	138	20	233
Wilkes	1599	447	533	161	248	63	472
Yancey	1045	152	207	44	116	28	188
	27,282	4906	6359	1822	3042	976	5840

ASHE COUNTY
CONFEDERATE SERVICE 1861-1865

	Company	Regiment	Total Men In Service	Total Wounds	Captured	Killed in Battle	Non-Combat Deaths	Died in Union Prisons	Total Deaths
1	A	9th (1st Cav)	175	22	37	9	20	4	33
2	D	5th Battalion	112	0	18	1	10	0	11
3	C	McRaes Cav.	104	N/A	N/A	N/A	N/A	N/A	0
4	A	26th	231	72	86	32	31	7	70
5	A	34th	152	61	39	14	20	7	41
6	A	37th	202	84	66	44	42	6	92
7	L	58th	150	29	31	7	15	10	32
8	M	58th	46	N/A	N/A	N/A	3	N/A	3
9	D	69th	42	N/A	N/A	N/A	N/A	N/A	N/A
10	D	70th	10	N/A	N/A	N/A	N/A	N/A	N/A
			1224	268	277	107	141	34	282

BUNCOMBE COUNTY
CONFEDERATE SERVICE 1861-1865

	Company	Regiment	Total Men In Service	Total Wounds	Captured	Killed in Battle	Non-Combat Deaths	Died in Union Prisons	Total Deaths
1	G	9th (1st Cav)	162	13	38	8	8	6	22
2	C	65th (6th Cav)	47	1	11	1	1	2	4
3	B	69th (7th Cav)	118	1	4	1	0	0	1
4	C	69th (7th Cav)	101	0	4	0	1	0	1
5	F	69th (7th Cav)	53	0	2	1	0	0	1
6	I	69th (7th Cav)	7	N/A	N/A	N/A	N/A	N/A	0
7	K	69th (7th Cav)	27	N/A	6	N/A	N/A	N/A	0
8	E	1st (6 Months)	137	N/A	N/A	N/A	4	N/A	4
9	K	11th	128	35	54	15	16	13	44
10	F	14th	142	44	24	15	22	5	42
11	F	16th	119	46	29	11	21	4	36
12	H	25th	83	16	13	10	9	2	21
13	I	25th	175	50	33	11	26	1	38

	Com-pany	Regiment	Total Men In Service	Total Wounds	Captured	Killed in Battle	Non-Combat Deaths	Died in Union Prisons	Total Deaths
14	K	25th	125	31	21	12	18	1	31
15	C	29th	186	29	45	5	23	10	38
16	H	29th	162	21	46	5	18	7	30
17	D	39th	123	19	17	6	19	1	26
18	F	39th	68	5	5	3	8	1	12
19	G	39th	83	8	10	1	12	0	13
20	A	60th	126	22	13	7	19	2	28
21	C	60th	114	12	15	10	15	3	28
22	E	60th	131	20	13	9	20	5	34
23	F	60th	122	16	13	6	19	4	29
24	K	60th	150	21	16	8	30	3	41
25	A	70th	57	N/A	N/A	N/A	N/A	N/A	N/A
			2746	410	432	145	309	70	524

BURKE COUNTY
CONFEDERATE SERVICE 1861-1865

	Company	Regiment	Total Men In Service	Total Wounds	Captured	Killed in Battle	Non-Combat Deaths	Died in Union Prisons	Total Deaths
1	F	41st (3rd Cav)	134	9	12	3	6	4	13
2	C	5th Battalion	65	0	19	0	2	0	2
3	E	McRae's Cav.	111	1	0	0	2	0	2
4	G	1st (6 Months)	125	0	0	0	5	0	5
5	D	6th	201	59	96	21	20	7	48
6	E	6th	109	41	36	11	15	5	31
7	B	11th	56	17	33	4	8	5	17
8	D	11th	134	37	67	17	21	10	48
9	E	16th	171	39	58	24	30	1	55
10	K	35th	93	20	32	7	15	0	22
11	B	46th	160	60	19	15	33	4	52
12	B	54th	40	10	23	4	6	3	13
13	A	70th	51	N/A	N/A	N/A	N/A	N/A	N/A
			1450	293	395	106	163	39	308

CALDWELL COUNTY
CONFEDERATE SERVICE 1861-1865

	Company	Regiment	Total Men In Service	Total Wounds	Captured	Killed in Battle	Non-Combat Deaths	Died in Union Prisons	Total Deaths
1	B	11th	56	17	33	4	8	4	16
2	A	22nd	204	116	50	28	27	5	60
3	F	26th	242	91	82	41	31	9	81
4	I	26th	271	63	74	24	30	9	63
5	E	58th	325	37	39	13	24	18	55
6	H	58th	174	29	21	11	15	4	30
			1272	353	299	121	135	49	305

CATAWBA COUNTY
CONFEDERATE SERVICE 1861-1865

	Company	Regiment	Total Men In Service	Total Wounds	Cap-tured	Killed in Battle	Non-Combat Deaths	Died in Union Prisons	Total Deaths
1	A	12th	192	80	66	23	16	4	43
2	F	23rd	178	68	82	25	36	8	69
3	C	28th	213	97	97	43	33	12	88
4	E	32nd	157	41	65	22	14	9	45
5	F	32nd	141	26	58	9	16	15	40
6	K	35th	93	20	32	7	15	0	22
7	F	38th	132	39	41	14	15	5	34
8	K	46th	161	77	27	34	32	1	67
9	I	49th	140	59	56	19	26	1	46
10	E	57th	140	27	99	8	24	14	46
			1547	534	623	204	227	69	500

CHEROKEE COUNTY
CONFEDERATE SERVICE 1861-1865

	Company	Regiment	Total Men In Service	Total Wounds	Captured	Killed in Battle	Non-Combat Deaths	Died in Union Prisons	Total Deaths
1	A	19th (2nd Cav)	163	7	20	9	12	2	23
2	D	25th	149	25	22	12	15	3	30
3	A	29th	175	12	40	2	7	8	17
4	A	39th	129	19	10	2	18	1	21
5	C	39th	164	19	30	4	18	5	27
6	H	39th	67	7	6	4	9	2	15
7	H	69th	106	N/A	N/A	N/A	N/A	N/A	N/A
			953	89	128	33	79	21	133

CLAY COUNTY
CONFEDERATE SERVICE 1861-1865

	Company	Regiment	Total Men In Service	Total Wounds	Captured	Killed in Battle	Non-Combat Deaths	Died in Union Prisons	Total Deaths
1	F	65th (6th Cav)	122	0	21	2	1	4	7
2	G	25th	91	23	17	11	11	2	24
3	E	39th	135	18	24	4	13	2	19
4	B	62nd	106	48	4	0	4	15	19
			454	89	66	17	29	23	69

CLEVELAND COUNTY
CONFEDERATE SERVICE 1861-1865

	Company	Regiment	Total Men In Service	Total Wounds	Captured	Killed in Battle	Non-Combat Deaths	Died in Union Prisons	Total Deaths
1	E	12th	191	51	43	27	22	1	50
2	D	14th	155	38	43	26	44	6	76
3	C	15th	206	59	50	20	38	4	62
4	H	28th	198	45	39	30	43	3	76
5	F	34th	171	59	52	40	16	6	62
6	H	34th	141	36	38	16	23	7	46
7	I	38th	129	34	28	19	22	5	46
8	B	49th	111	31	43	12	2	2	16
9	G	49th	166	35	60	18	27	5	50
10	C	55th	144	43	77	14	17	18	49
11	D	55th	152	55	63	18	16	13	47
12	F	55th	145	56	56	21	25	10	56
13	F	56th	143	45	48	20	29	3	52
			2052	587	640	281	324	83	688

HAYWOOD COUNTY
CONFEDERATE SERVICE 1861-1865

	Company	Regiment	Total Men In Service	Total Wounds	Captured	Killed in Battle	Non-Combat Deaths	Died in Union Prisons	Total Deaths
1	E	69th (7th Cav)	67	0	11	0	0	0	0
2	L	16th	158	25	5	10	19	1	30
3	C	25th	193	48	22	12	22	1	35
4	F	25th	131	29	15	9	20	0	29
5	E	29th	162	16	38	8	24	7	39
6	A	62nd	176	5	74	0	10	26	36
7	C	62nd	144	2	64	0	7	23	30
8	I	62nd	174	1	50	0	3	20	23
9	C	69th	106	N/A	N/A	N/A	N/A	N/A	N/A
10	E	69th	141	N/A	N/A	N/A	N/A	N/A	N/A
11	C	70th	52	N/A	N/A	N/A	N/A	N/A	N/A
			1504	126	279	39	105	78	222

HENDERSON COUNTY
CONFEDERATE SERVICE 1861-1865

	Company	Regiment	Total Men In Service	Total Wounds	Captured	Killed in Battle	Non-Combat Deaths	Died in Union Prisons	Total Deaths
1	D	65th (6th Cav)	126	1	40	2	4	10	16
2	K	65th (6th Cav)	38	0	14	0	0	6	6
3	G	79th (7th Cav)	94	0	4	0	0	2	2
4	I	16th	141	76	29	22	23	4	49
5	A	25th	190	39	32	8	26	4	38
6	H	25th	83	15	13	10	8	2	20
7	G	35th	117	26	23	10	25	0	35
8	G	56th	193	34	40	26	13	2	41
9	D	60th	132	11	34	3	23	14	40
10	B	64th	160	7	48	0	7	19	26
11	C	70th	22	N/A	N/A	N/A	N/A	N/A	N/A
			1296	209	277	81	129	63	273

JACKSON COUNTY
CONFEDERATE SERVICE 1861-1865

	Com-pany	Regiment	Total Men In Service	Total Wounds	Cap-tured	Killed in Battle	Non-Combat Deaths	Died in Union Prisons	Total Deaths
1	A	16th	135	29	7	12	19	0	31
2	B	25th	182	43	26	17	24	3	44
3	F	29th	137	19	32	5	12	3	20
4	K	39th	95	19	8	3	2	0	5
5	G	62nd	92	0	47	0	2	20	22
6	H	62nd	102	4	96	2	2	23	27
7	*A	69th	125	N/A	N/A	N/A	N/A	N/A	N/A
8	*B	69th	117	N/A	N/A	N/A	N/A	N/A	N/A
9	F	69th	129	N/A	N/A	N/A	N/A	N/A	N/A
10	G	69th	70	N/A	N/A	N/A	N/A	N/A	N/A
			1184	114	216	39	61	49	149

★ These two companies include over two-hundred Cherokees.

MACON COUNTY
CONFEDERATE SERVICE 1861-1865

	Company	Regiment	Total Men In Service	Total Wounds	Captured	Killed in Battle	Non-Combat Deaths	Died in Union Prisons	Total Deaths
1	K	9th (1st Cav)	173	24	26	8	15	1	24
2	E	65th (6th Cav)	113	2	15	0	1	1	2
3	G	65th (6th Cav)	139	1	18	1	3	4	8
4	A	69th (7th Cav)	122	0	3	1	0	0	1
5	H	16th	132	38	47	11	18	6	35
6	G	25th	91	23	17	10	11	1	22
7	B	39th	147	41	17	10	23	3	36
8	I	39th	124	23	13	9	36	1	46
9	D	62nd	137	5	84	1	4	22	27
10	K	69th	89	N/A	N/A	N/A	N/A	N/A	N/A
			1267	157	240	51	111	39	201

MADISON COUNTY
CONFEDERATE SERVICE 1861-1865

	Company	Regiment	Total Men In Service	Total Wounds	Captured	Killed in Battle	Non-Combat Deaths	Died in Union Prisons	Total Deaths
1	A	5th Battalion	195	0	16	0	3	0	3
2	I	65th (6th Cav)	90	2	35	1	1	6	8
3	D	69th (7th Cav)	118	0	4	3	0	0	3
4	H	2nd Battalion	179	22	163	11	15	9	35
5	B	16th	236	30	35	6	15	1	22
6	D	29th	137	21	38	3	12	6	21
7	B	60th	107	19	23	5	24	6	35
8	I	60th	101	15	14	2	27	4	33
9	A	64th	177	2	44	1	14	10	25
10	C	64th	159	3	40	0	4	6	10
11	D	64th	151	3	41	0	5	15	20
12	F	64th	143	1	30	1	8	10	19
13	G	64th	176	2	20	1	6	5	12
			1969	120	503	34	134	78	246

McDOWELL COUNTY
CONFEDERATE SERVICE 1861-1865

	Company	Regiment	Total Men In Service	Total Wounds	Captured	Killed in Battle	Non-Combat Deaths	Died in Union Prisons	Total Deaths
1	K	65th (6th Cav)	37	0	14	0	0	5	5
2	E	6th	110	41	36	10	15	4	29
3	B	22nd	181	58	54	20	42	7	69
4	K	22nd	212	59	55	28	29	10	67
5	B	35th	136	32	29	10	22	1	33
6	A	49th	77	16	18	8	13	1	22
7	B	54th	40	10	23	4	6	3	13
8	F	58th	225	28	32	19	27	5	51
			1018	244	261	99	154	36	289

MITCHELL COUNTY
CONFEDERATE SERVICE 1861-1865

	Com-pany	Regiment	Total Men In Service	Total Wounds	Cap-tured	Killed in Battle	Non-Combat Deaths	Died in Union Prisons	Total Deaths
1	B	5th Battalion	92	0	22	1	4	0	5
2	I	29th	125	22	22	2	12	2	16
3	A	58th	254	37	5	11	21	2	34
4	B	58th	164	19	2	7	11	1	19
5	K	58th	136	16	4	2	11	0	13
			771	94	55	23	59	5	87

POLK COUNTY
CONFEDERATE SERVICE 1861-1865

	Company	Regiment	Total Men In Service	Total Wounds	Captured	Killed in Battle	Non-Combat Deaths	Died in Union Prisons	Total Deaths
1	K	16th	139	35	37	17	24	4	45
2	I	54th	115	13	44	5	23	5	33
3	G	60th	93	16	12	4	23	2	29
4	E	64th	118	3	27	0	11	4	15
			465	67	120	26	81	15	122

RUTHERFORD COUNTY
CONFEDERATE SERVICE 1861-1865

	Com-pany	Regiment	Total Men In Service	Total Wounds	Cap-tured	Killed in Battle	Non-Combat Deaths	Died in Union Prisons	Total Deaths
1	C	65th (6th Cav)	46	0	11	1	1	1	3
2	D	16th	156	32	26	22	34	3	59
3	G	16th	159	72	39	17	26	4	47
4	B	34th	169	36	48	18	40	6	64
5	C	34th	178	44	36	24	31	9	64
6	I	34th	169	50	42	8	27	5	40
7	A	49th	76	15	17	7	13	1	21
8	G	50th	153	2	7	1	23	3	27
9	I	50th	174	3	5	2	20	1	23
10	K	50th	144	1	2	2	19	2	23
11	I	56th	144	38	55	19	19	2	40
12	F	62nd	223	5	155	0	10	37	47
13	B	70th	98	N/A	N/A	N/A	N/A	N/A	N/A
14	C	70th	92	N/A	N/A	N/A	N/A	N/A	N/A
			1981	298	443	121	263	74	458

TRANSYLVANIA COUNTY CONFEDERATE SERVICE 1861-1865

	Company	Regiment	Total Men In Service	Total Wounds	Captured	Killed in Battle	Non-Combat Deaths	Died in Union Prisons	Total Deaths
1	C	65th (6th Cav)	46	0	11	1	1	2	4
2	H	69th (7th Cav)	36	N/A	N/A	N/A	N/A	N/A	N/A
3	E	25th	171	48	19	14	22	3	39
4	E	62nd	142	6	90	0	6	18	24
5	K	62nd	154	2	39	0	7	17	24
			549	56	159	15	36	40	91

WATAUGA COUNTY
CONFEDERATE SERVICE 1861-1865

	Company	Regiment	Total Men In Service	Total Wounds	Captured	Killed in Battle	Non-Combat Deaths	Died in Union Prisons	Total Deaths
1	D	9th (1st Cav)	170	27	36	11	19	3	33
2	B	37th	190	66	51	27	39	9	75
3	E	37th	186	66	86	26	37	4	67
4	D	58th	199	18	17	6	20	2	28
5	I	58th	145	22	16	5	20	2	27
6	M	58th	46	0	0	0	3	0	3
			936	199	206	75	138	20	233

WILKES COUNTY
CONFEDERATE SERVICE 1861-1865

	Company	Regiment	Total Men In Service	Total Wounds	Captured	Killed in Battle	Non-Combat Deaths	Died in Union Prisons	Total Deaths
1	B	1st	192	64	54	35	20	7	62
2	B	11th	56	17	33	4	8	4	16
3	C	26th	196	64	68	25	24	6	55
4	D	33rd	179	46	51	16	41	5	62
5	F	37th	204	61	79	26	38	8	72
6	F	52nd	217	78	80	15	44	15	74
7	K	53rd	127	29	39	12	22	8	42
8	E	54th	121	27	40	6	13	1	20
9	G	54th	145	30	66	7	29	5	41
10	B	55th	133	31	23	15	9	4	28
11	D	70th	29	N/A	N/A	N/A	N/A	N/A	N/A
			1599	447	533	161	248	63	472

YANCEY COUNTY
CONFEDERATE SERVICE 1861-1865

	Company	Regiment	Total Men In Service	Total Wounds	Captured	Killed in Battle	Non-Combat Deaths	Died in Union Prisons	Total Deaths
1	C	16th	152	41	44	11	25	2	38
2	B	29th	191	19	38	6	16	4	26
3	G	29th	116	13	32	10	13	3	26
4	K	29th	119	5	38	1	12	4	17
5	B	54th	40	10	23	4	6	3	13
6	C	58th	169	38	4	4	26	2	32
7	G	58th	258	26	28	8	18	10	36
			1045	152	207	44	116	28	188

Chapter Five

SLAVERY

A fundamental element in promoting the "mountain myth" is the issue of slavery. A visitor to the area will often hear a description or verbal account of our history that exculpates our ancestors from the charge of slavery. It is apparent to me that such descriptions were designed to disassociate our ancestors from this horrible crime. The local storyteller may describe our history as follows: "We didn't have much slavery here in western North Carolina. We had a lot of small yeoman farmers who had no interest in slavery." The follow-up might also include some supporting information: "That's why we had a lot of Unionism here; our people were against slavery." Thus the speaker uses "Unionism" to distance our ancestors from the dark stain on our history while indirectly promoting the Unionism myth.

Unfortunately, these claims are untrue on the first count and misrepresented on the Unionism issue. Western North Carolina families were substantially involved in slavery. It is true that circumstances here were different and that the plantation system never really took hold here. But still there was slavery and plenty of it. It is also clear that most of the issues and events impacting the rest of the South also played a pivotal and possibly an equal role in the mountains.

Perhaps the most outstanding work on the topic of slavery in our area is *Mountain Masters: Slavery and the Sectional Crisis in Western North Carolina* by John Inscoe. His important documentation of slavery in the mountains exposes the fact that the practice was more widespread here than one might think. As a percentage of the population slaves averaged about 12 percent in 1850 and 10 percent in 1860 in the western counties that Inscoe researched.[1] The problem is that four important western North Carolina counties were not included in his study. He did not include Polk, Rutherford, Cleveland, and Catawba counties. These counties had a higher percentage of slaves among their population. Had they been included, the overall percentages would have been somewhat higher.

There are several other less obvious reasons that lend credibility to the assertion that mountain people were significantly involved in slavery. Most people were at least partially engaged in the slave economy. Many smaller families may not have owned slaves but they may have contracted for slave labor to do their worst farm jobs, or they did other business with slave owners. Zeb Vance was an attorney, but he owned six slaves according to the 1860 U.S. Census. One might suspect that he was involved in the contracting of slave labor.

The practice of slavery was also interwoven into other parts of the economy. Younger families tended not to own slaves according to the record. What the record does not reveal is that many of the younger families did expect to inherit them.

Slavery was also mixed in with charitable causes. In modern times charitable groups are known to approach the more affluent members of the community and solicit donations of cash. In pre-Civil War mountain communities the contributions often came in the form of slave labor.

While it is true that large slaveholders were rare in the mountains, many families owned one or several. You might hear someone describe such slaves as "house slaves." While we might wish that to be true, such descriptions are probably euphemistic. The reality is that in most cases where the slave holdings were small, the slave or slaves were farm slaves.

That is to say, they were likely burdened with the worst work a farm had to offer.

It wasn't just those who stuck to the Confederate cause who had an interest in slavery. Alexander Hamilton Jones's own relatives were engaged in the practice. According to the U.S. Census Slave Index of 1860, W.W. Jones owned one slave; Levi Jones, two; Robert Jones, Sr., two; Robert Jones, Jr., two; and James Jones also owned two slaves.[2] Most of these men went into the Union army.

The full extent of such involvement may never be known. It is also apparent that some white families did not agree with the practice of slavery. There were more than twelve hundred free blacks listed in the 1850 census and more than fifteen hundred listed in the 1860 census. Someone was freeing slaves, albeit slowly.

There has been a widespread misconception that the practice of slavery was not fully established in the mountains. The census records of 1850, 1860, and documentation of the period prove otherwise.

Perhaps the most puzzling aspect of this part of the story is the fact that some black men served in the Confederate army in some capacity. What role they played and how they were treated remains a topic of debate among scholars, but there is no doubt that some did serve as Confederates. In 1929 there were still twelve people receiving a Confederate pension from the state of North Carolina residing in Henderson County. Two of the twelve were African-American.[3]

REFERENCES
1. Inscoe, John C., *Mountain Masters: Slavery and the Sectional Crisis in Western North Carolina,* The University of Tennessee Press, Knoxville, Tennessee, 1989, pages 60-61.
2. United States Census of 1860, Henderson County, North Carolina Slave Index.
3. "12 Proposed for Pensions," *Times-News*, Hendersonville, North Carolina, July 4, 1929, page 1.

Chapter Six

—— THE MONUMENTS ——

There have been two recent articles published by *The North Carolina Historical Review* addressing Civil War monuments. The first is "In Memory of the Confederate Dead: Masculinity and the Politics of Memorial Work in Goldsboro, North Carolina," by Amy Crow, and "Evidence of Woman's Loyalty, Perseverance, and Fidelity: Confederate Soldiers' Monuments in North Carolina, 1865-1914," by Tom Vincent. I bring these articles to the reader's attention in order to provide an alternative view.

Crow and Vincent have an entirely different view of the monuments and the motivation to put them there than I do. Both writers seem to see a lot of subliminal motivations in the minds of monument builders that I don't see.[1] They use phrases like "elite white women" a lot.[2] The basic theme of both articles is that the monuments were part of a grand social, political, and clandestine plan to maintain white supremacy and male dominance in the postwar South. One gets the impression from these articles that racism was somehow a primary motivation. Early in my life I knew some of those women; they just didn't seem "elite" to me. I'm confident that most of them would have been appalled if they had known that they would be so labeled.

While I agree that political and social activity in the postwar South cannot be separated from the shameful development of discrimination and racism that evolved, I seriously doubt that the monument movement had much to do with it. As with any project where more than one person is involved, there are probably as many motivations as there are people. Considering the time, many of the citizens involved probably were "racist" but I don't think that had much to do with why they wanted to put up monuments.

In the case of Confederate monuments I think it is possible that most of those involved in organizing, funding, and constructing such monuments did so simply to honor the service and sacrifice of law-abiding men who did what they thought was right at the time. These men were their ancestors and they did sacrifice considerably. Putting up monuments is an age-old practice that is seen in almost all cultures following almost all wars. In the end the monuments usually outlive their creators and their issues.

In the later part of the nineteenth century and the first half of the twentieth century southern historians often presented a glamorous and radically unrealistic view of the South's involvement in the American Civil War. Many modern revisionist historians are equally unrealistic with a view from the opposite pole. The truth probably lies somewhere in between.

For the purposes of this study I've photographed most of the Civil War monuments in western North Carolina. The meaning of these monuments seems obvious to me but others may see something else. I read the words carved in stone and bronze and accept them without searching for conspiracy. "To Our Confederate Dead," some of them read.

When evaluating the Civil War in the mountains one should consider that these stone and bronze messages represent the voices of our ancestors. While it must be recognized that this ancestral connection does not include everyone, it does include significant portions of the population. There is one Union monument in the mountain region located in Henderson County but it is contemporary. The Confederate monument in Wilkes County is also contemporary. Only the monuments dedicated before World War II were witnessed and admired by some of those whose lives were touched by the flames of Civil War.

Most of them were conceived, constructed, and dedicated by the people who lived it and their immediate descendants. They wanted to recognize the events and those who sacrificed. One can argue that the cause was bad, that the monuments promote something negative, or just about anything else. When considering them en masse it is difficult to argue that the monuments of western North Carolina indicate anything other than past Confederate allegiance.

REFERENCES
1. Crow, Amy, "In Memory of the Confederate Dead: Masculinity and the Politics of Memorial Work in Goldsboro, North Carolina, 1894-1895," *The North Carolina Historical Review*, Vol. LXXXIII, North Carolina Office of Archives and History, Department of Cultural Resources, Raleigh, North Carolina, 2006, page 33.
2. Vincent, Tom, "Evidence of Woman's Loyalty, Perseverance, and Fidelity: Confederate Soldiers' Monuments in North Carolina, 1865-1914," *The North Carolina Historical Review,* Vol. LXXXIII, North Carolina Office of Archives and History, Department of Cultural Resources, Raleigh, North Carolina, 2006, page 63.

BUNCOMBE COUNTY
2,746 names on Confederate roster; at least 524 died in service; located downtown in Asheville, North Carolina

BUNCOMBE COUNTY VANCE MONUMENT
Dedicated to North Carolina Confederate Colonel and Confederate War Governor Zebulon Baird Vance; located downtown in Asheville, North Carolina

BURKE COUNTY
1,450 names on Confederate roster; at least 208 died in service; located on town square, Morganton, North Carolina

CALDWELL COUNTY
*1,272 names on Confederate roster; at least 305 died in service;
located downtown in Lenoir, North Carolina*

CATAWBA COUNTY
*1,547 names on Confederate roster; at least 500 died in service;
located on town square in Newton, North Carolina*

THE MONUMENTS 123

CHEROKEE RESERVATION THOMAS MONUMENT
Dedicated to Cherokee Chief and Confederate Colonel William Holland Thomas; located on U.S. Highway 441 outside Cherokee, North Carolina

CLEVELAND COUNTY
2,052 names on Confederate roster; at least 688 died in service; located downtown in Shelby, North Carolina

THE MONUMENTS 125

HAYWOOD COUNTY
1,504 names on Confederate roster; at least 222 died in service; located downtown in Waynesville, North Carolina

HAYWOOD COUNTY STRINGFIELD AND THOMAS MONUMENTS
Monuments marking the graves of Confederate Colonels William Stringfield and William Holland Thomas; located in Greenhill Cemetery, Waynesville, North Carolina

HENDERSON COUNTY
*1,296 names on Confederate roster; at least 273 died in service;
located downtown in Hendersonville, North Carolina*

JACKSON COUNTY
*1,184 names on Confederate roster; at least 149 died in service;
located downtown in Sylva, North Carolina*

MACON, CLAY, AND CHEROKEE COUNTIES
*2,674 names on Confederate roster; at least 403 died in service;
located downtown in Franklin, North Carolina*

THE MONUMENTS

MADISON COUNTY
1,969 names on Confederate roster; at least 246 died in service; one of three Dixie Highway/Robert E. Lee monuments; the one in this photograph is located downtown in Marshall, North Carolina

RUTHERFORD COUNTY
*1,981 names on Confederate roster; at least 458 died in service;
located downtown in Rutherfordton, North Carolina*

WILKES COUNTY
1,599 names on Confederate roster; at least 472 died in service; located on the property of The Old Wilkes Jail, Wilkesboro, North Carolina

WILKES COUNTY GORDON MONUMENT
Monument marking the grave of Confederate General James B. Gordon; located at Saint Paul's Episcopal Church cemetery, Wilkesboro, North Carolina

HENDERSON COUNTY-UNION
At least 130 Henderson County men entered Federal service after September 1, 1863. Located in Etowah, North Carolina, on the grounds of Henderson County Library, Etowah Branch, the monument was dedicated in 1985.

BUNCOMBE COUNTY
*Monument to Confederate dead; located on the grounds of the
Smith-McDowell House in Asheville, North Carolina*

Chapter Seven

—— THE ANTI-CONFEDERATES ——

One of the most misjudged pieces of evidence regarding the question of Unionism is the meaning of a Federal army uniform. The fact that a man wore a blue uniform may mean something else entirely. In many cases the men in blue really represented a "third side" in western North Carolina and elsewhere in the South. There should be classifications of Union, Confederate and anti-Confederate used when categorizing loyalties here.

In the beginning there was only the Union. By the end of 1860 the movement toward secession was well under way but Unionism was still in the majority. After Fort Sumter and Lincoln's call for troops almost everyone was a Confederate. After the passage of the Confederate Conscription Act in April of 1862 a small but growing group of objectors began to emerge. Ordinary people who probably supported the Confederacy in general did not plan to leave their homes and fight.

The battlefield slaughters of 1862 brought increasing pressure upon the Confederate army for more manpower. Reports of these horrific battles also increased the reluctance of men to serve. Battles such as Gains Mill, Frazier Farm, Malvern Hill, Gettysburg, and Fredericksburg all brought news of death and mutilation to many mountain families. Men lucky enough to survive came home on wounded leave with tales of huge bloody battles. Many of these men were armless, legless, or blind.

One-year enlistments were changed to three years or for the duration of the war. Families who supported the Confederacy originally began to resent the government when it became necessary for the army to take their fathers, brothers, and sons against their will. Most of them just wanted to be left alone.

The horrors of war and constant fighting continued to shake southern confidence on both the battlefield and on the home front. Almost every family had lost loved ones. Farmers away at war couldn't help with crops and the Union blockade cut off outside supplies. Families were threatened with starvation and hardship. Desertion became a widespread problem by the end of 1862. Sometimes Confederate deserters resorted to crime in order to survive. The victims of these crimes were often the families of Confederate soldiers.

The Confederate Conscription Act originally called all white males from eighteen to thirty-five. As the manpower shortage grew increasingly threatening to the Confederate cause the age limit was raised first from thirty-five to forty then to forty-five.[1] With each change in the law more and more mountain men became threatened by conscription.

As the carnage continued the demand for more manpower drove the Confederate conscription effort to the limit. As the war raged on, desertion threatened to undermine the South's ability to continue the conflict. Deserters had bounties on their heads resulting in the capture of many. Some soldiers were induced or otherwise persuaded to return to duty. In some cases Confederate officers ordered a court marshal, which sometimes resulted in execution by firing squad.

One of the largest mass executions in U.S. history occurred on May 4, 1864, in Dalton, Georgia.[2,3] Fourteen men from western North Carolina were executed for desertion. General Joseph E. Johnston had taken over command of the Confederate Army of Tennessee in December of 1863. He issued a pardon for all those who had been absent illegally but the pardon came with a stern warning. The unauthorized trips home had to stop.

Men from the 58th and the 60th North Carolina Infantry Regiments were close enough to western North Carolina to walk home. They often did so without leave. In many cases some men were known to return to duty after such trips. When the problem persisted General Johnston felt that he had to make examples of these men. Those executed were: Alford T. Ball, Jacob A. Austin, Asa Dover, Joseph A. Gibbs, Wright Hutchings, Christopher C. Ledford, George F. McFalls, Michael Ward, Hiram Youngblood, E.F. Younts, and probably William R. Byers, Reuben Dellinger, Jesse Hase, and James Randal.[4]

This event sent the army reeling. Instead of having the desired effect Johnston's mass execution led to an even larger mass desertion. Hundreds were said to have deserted that night. One of the executed was a distant relative of mine.

Other executions had occurred in other places involving other units. The records document at least thirty-six western North Carolina Confederate soldiers who were executed by the Confederate army. While these executions were no doubt horrific, they were not illegal. Whether legal or not these executions had a strong impact on mountain families. Without a doubt these events alienated the families and friends of those killed.

Illegal execution also played a role. In January 1863 a group of about fifty Shelton Laurel men raided the town of Marshall in Madison County to obtain salt and other commodities that were in scarce supply.[5] Apparently, at least some of the men were drunk and disorderly. They broke into the home of Confederate Colonel Lawrence M. Allen and "molested" his wife. Allen's two children were in bed with scarlet fever. Some claims indicate that the children may have also experienced some sort of molestation. The two children died within a few days of the incident. Whatever went on that night may never be totally understood, but it was something that sent Allen and his comrades into a violent rage.

MADISON COUNTY
SHELTON LAUREL

The marker indicates that the victims were killed because they were "suspected of Unionism." Most of these men were in the Confederate army in 1862. These families didn't become "Unionists" until after the massacre. The incident converted many former "anti-Confederates" into "Unionists."

In a desperate attempt to obtain justice or revenge or both, Lt. Col. James Keith took a detachment from Allen's 64th North Carolina Infantry Regiment into Shelton Laurel and arrested thirteen men and boys. Confederate leaders claimed that Keith was supposed to take the prisoners to Tennessee to stand trial. Instead Keith marched them a short distance and summarily executed the men.[6]

Today the "Bloody Madison" event, as it has become known, is treated as normal Confederate conduct even though there is no other such incident recorded in western North Carolina Civil War history.

The N.C. Office of Archives and History has erected a sign on Shelton Laurel Creek stating that the Shelton Laurel men were executed because they were "Unionists." I believe this particular historical marker to be incorrect. The men in question may not have been true Unionists in the winter of 1863; they might have been just anti-Confederates. It was the Shelton Laurel massacre that turned these families into Unionists. Most of the men had been in the Confederate army up until the latter part of 1862. They were Confederate deserters for the most part by the time of the massacre. The serious threat from Confederate enforcement probably drove some into the Union army. In all probability they would have sat out the war if they had been left alone.

It didn't take long for mountain men to figure out that a good place to increase their chance of survival was in the Union army. There were also the added benefits of food, shoes, and bounty money if they joined the Union. If they went over to the other side they would be paid real money with real value. Federal enlistment bounties were paid in U.S. "greenbacks," instead of worthless Confederate script. It was often more than a poor man could turn down.

Once this avenue of escape was discovered and accepted by anti-Confederates, more and more men made the difficult decision to cross over. But most people in the area still considered it treason. Remarkably, most of the men in Union prisons still refused to join even though they were starving to death or dying of disease or exposure. By war's end 976 mountain men are documented to have died in Union custody. The fact that many mountain men chose the Union army instead of prison is not surprising; the amazing thing is that several thousand others refused.

By the middle of 1863 the label of anti-Confederate probably fit well with a substantial portion of the mountain population. In 1865 it was far too late for many, yet others continued to sign up with the Federal army. The records indicate that a number of the men in Union regiments who have been counted by historians as "loyal" to the Union did not join up until well after the war was over. Of the 1,636 documented Union men from western North Carolina counties 354, or 22 percent of the total, enlisted after January 1, 1865. Some of these men are documented as having enlisted in June, July, even October of 1865 or later. Another group of latecomers joined in the latter half of 1864. There are 327 men, or 20 percent, who fall into that category. Their desertion rate was high and their combat exposure low.

General Robert E. Lee surrendered the Confederate Army of Northern Virginia on April 9, 1865. General Joseph E. Johnston followed a few days later when he surrendered the Confederate Army of Tennessee. Everyone knew that the South had lost except Jefferson Davis and a few other deluded Confederate leaders. Where had these "loyal" Union men been for the last four years? Most of them had been in the Confederate army at least part of the time and anti-Confederates for another portion of the time.

REFERENCES
1. Robertson, James I., Jr., *Southern Historical Society Papers, 1876-1959,* Kraus International Publications, Millwood, New York, 1980, Vol. XLV.
2. Clark, James (letter), *The Haversack,* a monthly newsletter of the Civil War Roundtable of Dalton, Georgia, April 2002, Vol. XX, No.10.
3. Jordan, Weymouth T., and Louis H. Manarin, *North Carolina Troops, 1861-1865: A Roster,* North Carolina Office of Archives and History, Department of Cultural Resources, Raleigh, North Carolina, Vol. XIV, page 237.
4. Ibid, page 463.
5. Trotter, William R., *Bushwhackers: The Civil War in North Carolina, The Mountains,* John F. Blair, Winston-Salem, North Carolina, 1988, page 222.
6. Jordan, Weymouth T., and Louis H. Manarin, *North Carolina Troops, 1861-1865: A Roster,* North Carolina Office of Archives and History, Department of Cultural Resources, Raleigh, North Carolina, Vol. XV.

Chapter Eight

—— AFRICAN-AMERICANS ——

For the most part, past historical arguments have centered on white males.[1] There has been little attention paid to the African-American role. The evidence indicates that some former slaves from the region joined the Union army at the earliest opportunity. There were four North Carolina Union regiments that are recorded as being made up of men of "African descent."[2]

1st Regiment Heavy Artillery, A. D., later renamed 14th United States Colored Artillery

1st Regiment Infantry, A. D., later renamed the 35th United States Colored Troops

2nd Regiment Infantry, A. D., later renamed the 36th United States Colored Troops

3rd Regiment Infantry, A. D., later renamed the 37th United States Colored Troops

It is probable that most of these men were from eastern North Carolina or other areas outside western North Carolina. *A Compendium of the War of the Rebellion* by Fredrick H. Dyer lists a total of 3,156 white males in the Union army from the entire state of North Carolina. It is important to note that the number shown in Dyer's compendium included only North Carolina Union regiments. This total would not include any North Carolina men who may have served in other states or in the "galvanized" U.S. regiments. It is estimated that there were over five thousand North Carolina men of African descent in the Union army by the end of the war.[3] How many of those were from western North Carolina is unknown.

There were a few African-Americans serving in mostly white Union regiments. The record reveals at least seven "black" men in the 3rd North Carolina Mounted Infantry. All seven were detailed as "cooks."

If the story is not confusing enough, we have the question of black Confederates to add to the mix. Charles K. Barrow published *Forgotten Confederates* in 1995. It was a serious look at the issue noting numerous accounts of black Confederates. Some modern historians do not want to recognize that such men existed but the record proves otherwise.[4]

"Most of the Negroes had arms, rifles, muskets, sabers, Bowie knives, dirks, etc.," Union Capt. Isaac W. Heysinger wrote in an 1862 account of the Maryland campaign. He said there appeared to be thousands among the Confederate army.[5]

It is doubtful that there were thousands but there were some. Another question regarding black Confederates is what sort of role they played in the Confederate army. It is probable that they were given lesser roles than their white counterparts. It is also probable that most of the early black Confederates were slaves accompanying their masters to the front. But there are also documented cases of free blacks joining the Confederate cause. One such person was Butler Owen of Henderson County. He was a free black who enlisted in Confederate Company A of the 25th North Carolina Infantry Regiment in early 1861.

There is other evidence of black Confederates from western North Carolina. As referenced in Chapter Five, in 1929 there were only twelve people left in Henderson County still drawing a Confederate pension from the state of North Carolina. Two of the twelve were African-American.[6]

Despite the existence of a smattering of black Confederates it is likely that the vast majority of African-Americans were totally behind the Union effort. It is the opinion of the author that except for the rare white individual who refused to be conscripted by the Confederates or who went to the Union army early, the African-Americans were the only true Unionists in western North Carolina during the early war period.

REFERENCES
1. Jones, A. H., *Knocking at the Door*, McGill & Witherow, Printers and Stereotypers, Washington, D.C., 1866, page 35.
2. Dyer, Frederick H., *A Compendium of the War of the Rebellion,* The Dyer Publishing Company, Des Moines, Iowa, 1908, pages 199-200.
3. Ibid.
4. "Whether blacks fought beside whites in Confederate Army is gray area," (AP), *Asheville Citizen-Times*, Feb. 21, 1999, page A4.
5. Ibid.
6. "12 proposed for pensions," *Times-News*, Hendersonville, North Carolina, July 4, 1929, page 1.

Chapter Nine

―― THE AFTERMATH ――

As stated previously, the mythology in this story lies in exaggeration. Western North Carolina Union men have been overestimated while Confederate loyalty has been underestimated. The smallest clue of affiliation is usually attributed to Unionism regardless of conflicting indicators or underlying circumstances. Men who joined the Federal army long after Lee surrendered have been counted as Civil War Unionists.

Examples of a Unionism bias continue to emerge even in a contemporary environment. A "Roster of Union Troops of Henderson County" in *The Heritage of Henderson County, Volume I*[1], originally published in 1985, contains the names of men who are supposed to represent Henderson County's Unionism during the war. A review of those listed indicates that more than half the names on that roster do not appear on the 1860 U.S. Census for Henderson County. Men might fail to appear on a census roll for a variety of reasons, but a similar study of Confederates from Henderson County shows a non-appear rate of only 20 percent. While the Henderson County Historical and Genealogical Society has done an excellent job with most of their research this roster is inaccurate. The society is dependent upon volunteers and sometimes the volunteers are biased. The goal from the beginning was probably to make the list as big as possible.

The title or label describing the roster gives the impression that over two hundred men from Henderson County were in the Union army. There is no information to tell the reader that almost none of these men went into the Union army until late, sometimes very late. The reader has no way of knowing that even if they really were from Henderson County they were probably in the Confederate army first and deserters second. Service in the Union army comes in a distance third. As strange as it may seem, some of these men had been recognized as Confederate heroes, having been through many battles. Some of these men had earned "the red badge of courage," as Confederates. Many of these late converts to Unionism joined to get out of Union prisons. At least sixty-eight Henderson County Confederates died in Union prisons rather than join Union service. Some of the men who went over to the Union side did so late in the war after the bounty payments reached an almost irresistible level and Confederate prospects hit bottom.

One fact alone nullifies the credibility of the Henderson County Roster: the last names of Grant, Hill, Jackson, and Payne were included without a first name, initial, or initials. These four men could have been anyone from anywhere. The inclusion of these names on the roster could not possibly have been documented or later verified but such inclusion does continue to inflate the myth.

It seems that in many cases the Union army was really the only reasonable option for some men toward the end. While western North Carolina men in Union service did have some combat experience it was very little compared to service in the Confederate army. They may have known that their chances of being ordered to charge into a hail of gunfire would be a lot less likely in the Union army.

The roster includes people who were either not from Henderson County or people who moved there after the war. Some men were added to the roster because they had a tombstone with a U.S. shield on it. Since government stones of that period don't usually include dates, such a criterion might accidentally result in including men who served all the way through the Spanish-American War. Beginning with World War I, a new type of stone was introduced. It should also be noted that for the purpose of compiling my roster of Union men I used the military records. The Blythes, who were in Henderson County by the time of the war, and other Henderson County Union converts, may appear on the Buncombe County or other county roster because the individual army record has a blank to fill in which reads "where born." Where they were living at the time of the war is not always easily discernable.

Another decision made by the compilers, which increased the size of the roster but led to more mistakes, was to use a special census. The Henderson County researchers who compiled their list included men found on the rolls of the special census taken in 1890. The purpose of the census was to identify all Civil War veterans still receiving a pension. A person living in Henderson County in 1890 could have been anywhere during the war and may or may not have been a "local" at the time.

One of the more unfortunate examples involves Hendersonville *Times-News* columnist Stephen Black. Black, a distant relative of mine, set out to tell what he believed was an accurate story of Unionism here in western North Carolina. He fell into the same traps that others, including the author, have fallen into. Everyone seems to have accepted it.

Black posted his column in the May 29, 2004, edition of the *Times-News*. He cited some sources including *The Heart of Confederate Appalachia: Western North Carolina in the Civil War* by John Inscoe and Gordon McKinney. This work is an excellent study of the period but it does not challenge the usual view of Unionism here. Inscoe and McKinney had not actually counted these men; they simply cited the count by Alexander Hamilton Jones that was discussed in Chapter Two of this work. Black reached conclusions that they did not.

Perhaps the most inaccurate statement in Black's 2004 column was that

"Wilkes County, however, was practically all Union." Wilkes County sent sixteen hundred men to the Confederate army and they fought like demons for the South. Nearly one-third of these Wilkes men died in Confederate service. The individual combat record of Wilkes County Confederates is remarkable. The bulk of the Wilkes men marched with Confederate General Robert E. Lee in the Army of Northern Virginia. More than three times as many men from Wilkes County died in Confederate service than ever served in the Union army from Wilkes. After reading the individual stories of these Wilkes men I can confidently say that by today's standards about seventy-five Wilkes men would qualify as Congressional Medal of Honor nominees fighting for the Confederacy.

While it is true that at least 145 Wilkes men are known to have joined the Union army, most did so very late in the war. Wilkes County was a Confederate county from beginning to end. While Wilkes' Unionist activities beginning in late 1863 have led other historians to conclude that Wilkes was a "Union" county the evidence proves otherwise. With almost one-third of their men dead, probably another one-third blind, legless, armless, or otherwise physically maimed, and the final one-third under the thumb of the Union army and psychologically devastated, it's no wonder that few spoke out against this perception after the war.

The battle record of these Union troops does not demonstrate anything outstanding in the way of combat. Most of their casualties resulted from raiding activities or men shot while caught behind the lines. Even though there were few battle casualties among these men disease did take a terrible toll.

While it is difficult to judge the performance of any particular regiment, the battle history does help. There are two Confederate regiments that don't seem to compare favorably with the others. The 62nd North Carolina and the 64th North Carolina did not seem to accomplish much. The primary makeup of each unit was conscripts. The 62nd managed to get captured en masse at Cumberland Gap in September of 1863. Some of them joined the Union army but many others refused.

Substantial numbers of these men died in Union custody. The 64th North Carolina is forever tainted by the Shelton Laurel massacre and its aftermath. There is little evidence to distinguish the 62nd and the 64th as active combat units.

For the Union units the picture is reasonably clear. Col. George W. Kirk was hailed by Union leaders as a hero for leading the 3rd North Carolina Mounted Infantry Regiment (Union) on a raid deep into Confederate territory in June of 1864. The target was Confederate Camp Vance located just outside Morganton, North Carolina, and the railroad terminus located there.

While the raid may have seemed dangerous on the surface, it is clear that Kirk knew there was no one defending the camp except young boys under age seventeen. The camp's regular guard had been sent to the front due to the extreme manpower shortage in the Confederate army.[2] Due to local intelligence Kirk knew he would meet little or no resistance. Once his presence was discovered and serious opposition mobilized, Kirk and his "home Yankees" wisely retreated to Union lines. Still there was some combat encountered on the retreat and Kirk himself was wounded in the arm.

It was during this raid and others like it that Kirk's reputation as a criminal emerged. All manner of rape, robbery, and plunder is attributed to these Union regiments by many Confederate accounts. On the retreat from the raid on Camp Vance, Kirk ordered his men to lie on their stomachs while ordering the young boys captured on the raid to stand in front of his line.[3] Indiscriminate crime and use of these boys as human shields earned Kirk and his men extreme enmity that lasted for decades.

While looking at the record of Stoneman's Cavalry and the North Carolina mountain men traveling with him, one must consider the leadership of General Alvan C. Gillem. Gillem was Stoneman's divisional commander and he was placed in full command when Stoneman departed from the field and his cavalry in mid-April 1865. The men of the Second Brigade of Stoneman's Cavalry were organized into three regiments, the 8th, 9th, and 13th Tennessee Cavalry.[4] These regiments, made up of Tennessee and North Carolina mountain men, were considered Gillem's men.

Gillem had served as provost marshal of the state of Tennessee prior to taking a cavalry command in 1863. He led a sizable force into east Tennessee beginning in April 1864. He worked the area for a time unopposed. In the fall of 1864 Confederate General John Breckenridge lead an offensive into the area. When Gillem and his men heard of the approaching Confederates a hasty retreat was ordered. Union soldiers began to panic as they scrambled to get out of the area. Weapons, food, and other accoutrements were left strewn along the escape route. The panic among Gillem's men was so extreme that Union General Ammen stated that "his cavalry ran over the infantry I sent to support him."[5] The event is still known in east Tennessee as "Gillem's stampede."[6]

An extensive study of Gillem and his men on Stoneman's raid reveals a most undistinguished record. There were four thousand men in three brigades of cavalry under Stoneman's command. The First Brigade was commanded by Col. William J. Palmer of Pennsylvania. The record indicates that Palmer's brigade conducted themselves properly, and the men of the Second Brigade (Gillem's men) and Third Brigade did not. Since Gillem was divisional commander his men were placed under the command of Gen. S. B. Brown and sometimes Col. John K. Miller, but they were still Gillem's men. The conduct of some of these men was criminal as described by their own accounts.[7]

Understanding the professionalism of Palmer helps understand the seriousness of his actions when he communicated with headquarters. Late in the war he wrote the adjutant-general at Stoneman's headquarters in Knoxville, Tennessee, regarding Gillem's men. "…officers for the most part have lost all control over their men. A large number of men and some of the officers devote themselves almost exclusively to pillaging and destroying property."[8]

The overwhelming sacrifice of Confederates would create emotional stress and conflict between the ex-Confederate majority and the men who made the decision to go over to the Union side. The remnants of such conflict may still exist in some mountain counties.

Conduct that Southerners often perceived as criminal during the war led to conflict after the war.[9] Initially the odds were heavily in the Unionists' favor, but with the election of 1870 the odds shifted overwhelmingly in the favor of ex-Confederates. Many families of men who had gone over banded together with others who had done the same. These folks were not held in the highest esteem by most of the population.

In many of the smaller mountain counties you may hear locals describe one part of the county as having been "Union" during the Civil War. The more likely reason for the sectional Union identity would have occurred postwar. Union families banded together for security reasons and tended to collect in certain areas of any given county. If one were living in town among a devastated, bitter, and hostile ex-Confederate majority, it would probably feel more comfortable out in the countryside with others in the same social and political category.

In some counties like-minded brethren crossed over from east Tennessee and settled with their friends and relatives. As the social and political process worked out differences between folks on all sides the mountaineers began the slow progression toward a peaceful coexistence. For practical reasons ex-Confederates joined in on the advantages of being Republican. In counties like Mitchell a combination of those who had joined the Union army, other Union veterans from east Tennessee, and ex-Confederates looking for opportunity formed the basis for a dominant Republican Party, which still exists today. But Mitchell County was not a Union county during the Civil War.

In some counties ex-Confederates may have made deals, committing to switch to the Republican Party, in exchange for a promise that all occupying troops would be withdrawn.

For better or worse western North Carolina was a bastion of the Confederacy during the Civil War. President Lincoln once asked his cabinet, "If you call a dog's tail a leg, how many legs does a dog have?" They all responded that the correct answer would be five.

"No," said Lincoln. "Calling a dog's tail a leg does not make it so." Such is the case for Unionism in western North Carolina; people have been describing a lot of tails as legs for nearly a century and a half. Some mountain men went into the Union army late in the war. Their service and sacrifice do not compare to that of their Confederate counterparts. There was some Unionism here but not nearly as much as we've been led to believe.

REFERENCES
1. *The Heritage of Henderson County, North Carolina, Vol. I,* Henderson County Genealogical and Historical Society, The Reprint Company, Publishers, Spartanburg, South Carolina, 2003, page 23.
2. Hilderman, Walter C., III, *They Went into the Fight Cheering! Confederate Conscription in North Carolina,* Parkway Publishers, Boone, North Carolina, 2005, pages 185-186.
3. Bumgarner, Matthew, *Kirk's Raiders: A Notorious Band of Scoundrels and Thieves,* Piedmont Press, Hickory, North Carolina, 2000, page 41.
4. Van Noppen, Ina Woestemeyer, *Stoneman's Last Raid,* North Carolina State University Print Shop, Raleigh, North Carolina, 1961, page 4.
5. Bumgarner, Matthew, *Kirk's Raiders: A Notorious Band of Scoundrels and Thieves,* Piedmont Press Hickory, North Carolina, 2000, page 51.
6. Post-Civil War, Sesquicentennial Edition, *Citizen-Tribune,* Morristown, Tennessee, April 23, 2005, page C-1.
7. Scott, Samuel W., and Samuel P. Angel, *History of the Thirteenth Regiment Tennessee Volunteer Cavalry, USA,* P.W. Ziegler & Company, Philadelphia, Pennsylvania, 1903, page 242.
8. *The War of the Rebellion: The Official Records of the Confederate and Union Armies,* Government Printing Office, Washington, D.C., 1880, Series 1, Vol. XLIX, Part I, page 550.
9. Arrowood, Virgil N., *Grandpa Fought on Three Sides,* Birco Publishing, Gladstone, Michigan, 1990, page 58.

Bibliography

Arrowood, Virgil N. *Grandpa Fought on Three Sides*. Gladstone, MI: Birco Publishing, 1990.

Arthur, John Preston. *Western North Carolina: A History from 1730 to 1913*. Reprint, Johnson City, TN: The Overmountain Press, 1996.

Barrett, John G. *The Civil War in North Carolina*. Chapel Hill: University of North Carolina Press, 1963.

_____. *North Carolina as a Civil War Battleground, 1861-1865*. Raleigh: Division of Archives and History, North Carolina Department of Cultural Resources, 1991.

Blackmun, Ora. *Western North Carolina: Its Mountains and Its People to 1880*. 2nd ed. Boone, NC: Appalachian Consortium Press, 1980.

Boatner, Mark M. III, ed. *The Civil War Dictionary*. New York: Vintage Books, 1991.

Bumgarner, Matthew. *Kirk's Raiders: A Notorious Band of Scoundrels and Thieves*. Hickory, NC: Piedmont Press, 2000.

Catton, Bruce. *The American Heritage New History of the Civil War*. Edited by James M. McPherson and Noah Andre Trudeau. New York: Viking, 1996.

Clark, James. Letter to Martha, 16 June 1864. *The Haversack*, Vol. XX, No. 10. Dalton, GA: April 2002.

Clark, Walter, ed. *Histories of the Several Regiments and Battalions from North Carolina in the Great War, 1861-1865*. 5 vols. Goldsboro, NC: Nash Brothers, Book and Job Printers, 1901.

Compiled Service Records of the First through the Sixth U.S. Volunteer Infantry. National Archives of the United States. Record Group No. 94, Microfilm No. 1017, 1978.

The Confederate Soldier in the Civil War. Fairfax, VA: The Fairfax Press, 1977.

Cotton, William D. *Appalachian North Carolina: A Political Study, 1860-1889*. Chapel Hill: University of North Carolina, 1954.

Crow, Amy. "In Memory of the Confederate Dead: Masculinity and the Politics of Memorial Work in Goldsboro, North Carolina, 1894-1895." *The North Carolina Historical Review*, Vol. LXXXIII. Raleigh: North Carolina Office of Archives and History, Department of Cultural Resources, 2006.

Crow, Vernon H. *Storm in the Mountains: Thomas' Confederate Legion of Cherokee Indians and Mountaineers*. Cherokee, NC: Press of the Museum of the Cherokee Indian, 1982.

Current, Richard N., ed. *Encyclopedia of the Confederacy*. New York: Simon & Schuster, 1993.

Davis, George B., Leslie J. Perry, and Joseph W. Kirkley. *The Official Military Atlas of the Civil War*. New York: Barnes & Noble Books, 2003.

Dyer, Frederick H. *A Compendium of the War of the Rebellion*. Des Moines: The Dyer Publishing Company, 1908.

Eicher, David J. *The Longest Night: A Military History of the Civil War*. New York: Simon & Schuster, 2001.

Eighty Acres of Hell. The History Channel. A&E Television Networks, 2002.

FitzSimons, Frank L. *From the Banks of the Oklawaha*. 2nd ed. Hendersonville, NC: Golden Glow Publishing Co., 1977.

Freeman, Douglas Southall. *Cedar Mountain to Chancellorsville*, Vol. 2 of *Lee's Lieutenants*. New York: Charles Scribner's Sons, 1945.

_____. *R. E. Lee*. New York: Charles Scribner's Sons, 1934.

Guernsey, Alfred H. and Henry M. Alden. *Harper's Pictorial History of the Civil War*. Reprint, New York: Gramercy Books, 1996.

The Heritage of Henderson County, North Carolina, Vol. I, Spartanburg, SC: Henderson County Genealogical and Historical Society, The Reprint Company, Publishers, 2003.

Hilderman, Walter C. III. *They Went Into the Fight Cheering!: Confederate Conscription in North Carolina*. Boone, NC: Parkway Publishers, Inc., 2005.

Hughes, Nathaniel C. *Bentonville: The Last Battle of Sherman and Johnston*. Chapel Hill: The University of North Carolina Press, 1996.

Inscoe, John C., and Gordon B. McKinney. *The Heart of Confederate Appalachia*. Chapel Hill: University of North Carolina Press, 2000.

Inscoe, John C. *Mountain Masters: Slavery and the Sectional Crisis in Western North Carolina*. Knoxville: The University of Tennessee Press, 1989.

Johnston, Frontis W., ed. *The Papers of Zebulon Baird Vance, Vol. 1*. Raleigh: State Department of Archives and History, 1963.

Jones, A. H. *Knocking at the Door*. Washington, D.C.: McGill & Witherow, Printers and Stereotypers, 1866.

Jordan, Weymouth T., and Louis H. Manarin. *North Carolina Troops, 1861-1865: A Roster*. North Carolina Office of Archives and History, Department of Cultural Resources, 1966.

Long, E. B. *The Civil War Day By Day*. Garden City, NY: Doubleday & Company, 1971.

Lossing, Benson J. *Mathew Brady's Illustrated History of the Civil War*. New York: Portland House, n.d.

Lowry, Thomas P., M.D. *The Story the Soldiers Wouldn't Tell: Sex in the the Civil War.* Mechaniscsburg, PA: Stackpole Books, 1994.
Manarin, Louis H. *A Guide to Military Organizations and Installations, North Carolina 1861-1865.* Raleigh: North Carolina Confederate Centennial Commission, 1961.
McCaslin, Richard B. *Portraits of Conflict.* Fayetteville: University of Alabama Press, 1997.
McPherson, James M. *For Cause & Comrades: Why Men Fought in the Civil War.* New York: Oxford University Press, 1997.
Moore, John W. *Roster of North Carolina Troops in the War Between the States.* Raleigh: Ashe & Gatlin, 1882.
Nelson, Christopher. *Mapping the Civil War: Featuring Rare Maps from the Library of Congress.* Golden, CO: Fulcrum Publishing, 1992.
Powell, William S., ed. *Dictionary of North Carolina Biography.* Chapel Hill: University of North Carolina Press, 1991.
Robertson, James I., Jr. *Southern Historical Society Papers, 1876-1959.* 52 Vols. New York: Kraus International Publications, Millwood, 1980.
Scott, Samuel W., and Samuel P. Angel. *History of the Thirteenth Regiment Tennessee Volunteer Cavalry USA.* Philadelphia: P.W. Ziegler & Company, 1903.
Speer, Allen Paul, ed. *Voices from Cemetery Hill: The Civil War Diary, Reports, and Letters of Colonel William Henry Asbury Speer (1861-1864).* Johnson City, TN: The Overmountain Press, 1997.
Time-Life Books, ed. *Arms and Equipment of the Confederacy.* Vol. 2 of *Echoes of Glory.* Alexandria, VA: Time-Life Books, 1996.
Trotter, William R. *Bushwackers: The Mountains.* Vol. 2 of *The Civil War in North Carolina.* Winston-Salem, NC: John F. Blair, 1988.
Van Noppen, Ina W. and John J. Van Noppen. *Western North Carolina Since the Civil War.* Boone, NC: Appalachian Consortium Press, 1973.
Van Noppen, Ina Woestemeyer, *Stoneman's Last Raid.* Raleigh: North Carolina State University Print Shop, 1961.
Vincent, Tom, "Evidence of Woman's Loyalty, Perseverance, and Fidelity: Confederate Soldiers' Monuments in North Carolina, 1865-1914." *The North Carolina Historical Review,* Vol. LXXXIII. Raleigh: North Carolina Office of Archives and History, Department of Cultural Resources, 2006.
The War of the Rebellion: The Official Records of the Confederate and Union Armies. Washington, D.C.: Government Printing Office, 1880.
Ward, Doris Cline, ed. *The Heritage of Old Buncombe County.* Asheville, NC: The Old Buncombe County Genealogical Society, 1981.
Watkins, Sam R. *Co. Aytch: A Confederate Memoir of the Civil War.* New York: Touchstone, 1997.
Wegner, Ansley Herring. *Phantom Pain.* Raleigh: Office of Archives and History, North Carolina Department of Cultural Resources, 2004.
Wellman, Manly Wade. *The Kingdom of Madison: A Southern Mountain Fastness and Its People.* Chapel Hill: The University of North Carolina Press, 1973.

_____. *Rebel Boast: First at Bethel, Last at Appomattox.* New York: Blue/Gray Books, 2000.

Wheeler, Richard. *Voices of the War: An Eyewitness History of the War Between the States.* New York: Thomas Y. Crowell Company, 1976.

Whitaker, Bruce C. *The Whitaker Family of Buncombe County, North Carolina and Genealogies of the Reed, Harper, and Wright Families.* Compiled by C. Bruce Whitaker. Asheville, NC: Ward Publishing Company, 1989.

Winslow, Hattie Lou, and Joseph R. H. Moore. *Camp Morton: 1861-1865 Indianapolis Prison Camp.* Indianapolis: Indiana Historical Society, 1995.

Yates, Richard E. *The Confederacy and Zeb Vance.* Tuscaloosa, AL: Thomas Yoseloff, 1962.

Personal Name Index

Abshire, Levi 69
Adams, Harper 69
Adams, William H. 69
Aldridge, Waitstel 60
Alexander, James E. 24
Allen, Adacrum 74
Allen, Andrew J. 74
Allen, Avery C. 53
Allen, Ervin 74
Allen, George 74
Allen, John 46
Allen, Lawrence M. 137, 138
Allen, Nathaniel 74
Allen, Perry 44
Allen, William 24
Allen, Young 74
Ammen, 149
Anders, David H. 74
Anders, Hiram 24
Anders, James B. 74
Anders, Jasper E. 74
Anders, John C. 24
Anders, William F. 74
Anderson, James F. 53
Anderson, John T. 53
Anderson, Riley 21
Anderson, Robert 24, 53
Anderson, William 24

Anderson, William W. 24
Angel, Samuel P. 151
Anitso, James 51
Arbury, Niner A. 45
Arklook, John 52
Arrowood, Edmund 24
Arrowood, Hughey G. 24
Arrowood, James 53
Arrowood, James P. 24
Arrowood, Virgil N. 151
Arrowood, Wesley 60
Arthurburn, Isaac 46
Arwood, Robert D. 24
Austin, Andrew T. 74
Austin, Clingman L. 74
Austin, Edward K. 74
Austin, Jacob A. 137
Austin, William A. 74
Austin, William H. 53
Bailey, Calvin 74
Bailey, Dobson 74
Bailey, Jasper S. 58
Bailey, Jefferson 74
Baker, James M. 21
Ball, Alford T. 137
Ball, Jeremiah C. 24
Ball, Manly 24
Ballard, James E. 64
Ballard, James R. 24

Ballard, John G. 64
Ballard, John K. 74
Ballard, John P. 53
Ballenger, James 24
Ballew, John 58
Ballew, Marion 74
Banks, Andrew J. 74
Banks, Berry P. 74
Banks, Edward 74
Banks, Ezekial 74
Banks, John 53
Banks, Samuel B. 74
Banks, William B. 74
Bare, Jessie 21
Barlow, Thomas J. 67
Barnett, John 53, 60
Barnett, Levi W. 24
Barnett, Simon 74
Barnett, Zachariah 24
Barrett, Christopher 24
Barrett, David 24
Barrett, George 41
Barrett, Jesse R. 24
Barrett, John E. 24
Barrow, Charles K. 142
Barton, Millington 66
Baynard, Martin 64
Beachboard, Alexander 24
Beachboard, Lorenzo D. 24

Bean, Enoch 37
Bean, Thomas 38
Bean, William W. 38
Beavers, James W. 24
Benfield, John H. 52
Benfield, Marion 37
Bennett, Abraham 74
Bennett, Archibald 74
Bennett, Baxter 74
Bennett, Jeremiah 75
Bennett, John 75
Bennett, John Jr. 75
Bennett, William 75
Benson, Alexander C. 51
Bias, Henry H. 64
Bigham, William P. 44
Billings, William 21
Bird, William 37
Bishop, Elbert 69
Black, Jesse L. 24
Black, Stephen 146
Black, William 60
Blackburn, Andrew 69
Blackburn, Collumbus F. 69
Blackburn, George F. 69
Blackburn, Thomas 21
Blackburn, William 69
Blackwell, Francis M. 46
Blackwell, John 46
Blackwell, Thomas 46
Blair, John F. 140
Blankenship, John Q. 69
Blankenship, Noah 53
Blythe, 146
Blythe, George F. 24
Blythe, Gilford I. 24
Blythe, Robert O. 25
Boon, Amos 75
Boon, Thomas 53
Borders, Drewy 69
Bowers, John F. 69
Bowers, William 69
Bowles, Melmoth 67

Bracher, Joseph 67
Brackens, James 25
Bradburn, Bluford 25
Bradburn, David F. 25
Bradburn, William 53
Bradford, Ervin 75
Bradford, John 75
Bradley, George W. 64
Bradley, John J. 64
Bradley, Thomas 58
Bradley, William T. 64
Bradshaw, George 51
Bradshaw, William 58
Brank, David V. 25
Brank, J. Washington 25
Brank, Mitchell A. 25
Brank, Winfield 25
Branum, Marion 45
Breckenridge, John 149
Briggs, Allison 75
Briggs, Garrett 25
Briggs, George W. 25
Briggs, Jasper 75
Briggs, John G. 25
Briggs, Wilson 25
Briton, Joseph 25
Brooks, Abner 53
Brooks, James 25
Brooks, John 53
Brookshire, Noah B. 69
Brown, Aaron 69
Brown, Adolphus E. 25
Brown, Ben 41
Brown, Doctor C. 64
Brown, Fielding 64
Brown, George H. 69
Brown, George W. 69
Brown, Isaac 41
Brown, John 25
Brown, Mark H. 69
Brown, S. B. 149
Brown, Thomas G. 40
Bryan, George W. 25
Bryan, Lewis (Levi) 25

Bryant, Allen M. 75
Bryant, James 75
Bryant, Nathan 75
Bryant, Thomas 75
Buchanan, Alexander 60
Buchanan, Caley 60
Buchanan, David M. 60
Buchanan, Green 60
Buchanan, Joseph 60
Buchanan, Joseph M. 60
Buchanan, William 60
Buchanan, William A. 60
Buckner, Alfred M. 25
Buckner, David 25
Buckner, George 25
Buckner, Harrison H. 25
Buckner, Harvey P. 25
Buckner, James M. 25
Buckner, James R. 53
Buckner, Jeremiah 25
Buckner, John H. 25
Buckner, Levi 75
Buckner, Nimrod 25
Buckner, Noah 25
Buckner, Philip 25
Buckner, Squire 25
Buckner, Stephen M. 25
Bullman, John 75
Bumgardner, David 21
Bumgarner, Emos S. 51
Bumgarner, Matthew 151
Burchett, Martin 69
Burgess, Aden H. 45
Burgess, James M. 41
Burgess, Solomon 69
Burgess, Thomas 21
Burleson, Daniel W. 26
Burleson, Greenberg 60
Burleson, James 75
Burleson, Oliver 60
Burleson, Samuel M. 26
Burleson, William 60
Burnett, Edward 26
Burns, Phillip 37

PERSONAL NAME INDEX

Burris, James 60
Burrison, John W. 75
Burton, Aaron J. 37
Burton, William 69
Butler, Alan 60
Butler, John 37
Butler, William 58
Byers, William R. 137
Byrd, Carson 60
Byrd, George 75
Byrd, Lace 75
Byrd, Mitchell 75
Byrd, Samuel 75
Byrd, William 69
Cagel, James H. 46
Cagle, James H. 46
Cairn, William H. 46
Caldwell, Andrew 45
Caldwell, David M. 45
Caldwell, Hamilton 45
Caldwell, Henry E. 26
Caldwell, James 53
Callaway, Thomas 75
Calloway, William 60
Calloway, William T. 52
Campbell, H. H. 67
Candler, James 26
Candler, Thomas J. 53
Cantrell, John 26
Cantrell, Levi 26
Capps, John D. 26
Capps, William 46
Capps, William M. 46
Carland, Franklin B. 26
Carpenter, Albert E. 38
Carpenter, Jonathan 60
Carpenter, Joshua 40
Carter, Abraham 26
Carter, John H. 26
Carter, William 26
Carter, William H. 26
Carter, Wilson 26
Carttrell, Valentine 46
Carup, James I. 46

Carver, James H. 58
Carver, John 58
Carver, John W. 58
Case, Andrew 26
Case, Elijah F. 26
Case, James M. 26
Case, Joshua F. 26
Case, William 26
Case, William L. 64
Cass, Allen R. 46
Caudill, Abner 69
Cercy, William 64
Chambers, Asia C. 45
Chambers, Joseph B. 26
Chambers, William K. 26
Chandler, John 75
Chapel, James W. 75
Childers, William 63
Chio-e-li, (Native American) 41
Church, Alfred 69
Church, G. W. 69
Church, Harrison 69
Church, Irvin 69
Church, John L. 69
Church, Jordan 69
Church, William F. 70
Citton, Kinsey 26
Citton, Silas C. 46
Clark, Adolphus 38
Clark, Detroit 38
Clark, Jacob 26
Clark, James 140
Clark, James E. 26
Clark, Noah 38
Clark, Richard M. 45
Clark, Samuel 26
Clark, Silas J. 75
Clark, Thaddeus W. 38
Clark, William H. 46
Clemens, James 26
Clemens, John 75
Clinton, James 75
Clinton, John 70

Cloud, Terrell 37
Club, William 26
Coates, Garrett 26
Cobb, Newton 38
Cockerham, Joseph 70
Cody, Gabriel 53
Cody, William 53
Coffey, Jesse Patterson 60
Coffey, Larkin 38
Cogdill, William A. 53
Coggins, Henry A. 26
Cole, Francis Marion 26
Cole, James H. 27
Cole, Thomas D. 27
Cole, William H. 27
Collins, George 64
Collins, Iriah 64
Collins, James T. 64
Collins, Solomon 38
Combs, Jefferson 27
Condrey, Gilford J. 46
Cook, Alfred W. 64
Cook, Benjamin 70
Cook, John H. 67
Cook, Thomas 37
Cooper, Joel W. 75
Cooper, John G. 75
Cooper, Lina 45
Cooper, William A. 75
Cordell, Adolphus 27
Cordell, Daniel 27
Cordell, James H. 75
Cordell, Soloman 27
Corn, Ezekiel W. 46
Corn, Hughes B. 27
Corn, Jessee 52
Cornutt, David E. 21
Cornutt, Isaac 21
Cornutt, Wiley 21
Correll, Henry 16
Cotton, William D. 88
Craig, Drewry 45
Crain, Albert 53
Cranford, Henry 76

Creswell, Francis M. 58
Crook, John P. 66
Cross, Joseph 46
Crow, Amy 115, 117
Crowder, Elijah B. 27
Crowder, Elsberry 27
Crowder, James A. 27
Crump, George W. 38
Crump, Henry 38
Curtis, Joshua C. 38
Curtis, Thomas 27
Dalton, James A. 58
Danner, Peter F. 67
Darnell, Morgan S. 70
Daugherty, John H. 21
Davis, Alfred N. 27
Davis, Andrew Jackson 53
Davis, David F. 27
Davis, George W. 27
Davis, Jackson 27
Davis, Jacob 76
Davis, James M. 27
Davis, Jefferson 140
Davis, John 27
Davis, John E. 27
Davis, Josiah 60
Davis, Minsey 27
Davis, Nathaniel, Jr. 53
Davis, Nesbet C. 70
Davis, Peter 27
Davis, Reuben 58
Davis, Robert A. 58
Davis, Silas 58
Davis, Stephen M. 76
Davis, Thomas M. 58
Davis, William 21
Day, Samuel 70
Day, William D. 38
Deal, Joseph A. 52
Deaver, William H. 27
Dellinger, Reuben 137
Devers, Shepard 27
Dickson, Charles R. 58
Dills, Francis M. 52

Dinkins, Lewis M. 38
Ditmore, Francis M. 43
Doby, George F. 76
Dockery, Alfred L. 53
Dockery, Elijah 27
Dockery, Franklin 53
Done, Morgan 27
Done, Zachariah T. 27
Dover, Asa 137
Dover, William 27
Dowell, Emerald 70
Dowell, James E. 70
Dowell, John L. 70
Downin, Samuel 76
Drake, Hezekiah 46
Drake, John B. 46
Drake, John H. 46
Drake, Nathan M. 46
Drake, Richard 46
Drake, William 46
Dryman, James 27
Du-Las-Ki, (Native American) 41
Dula, Elbert Sidney 27
Dunkin, Alfred J. 64
Dyer, Frederick H. 143
Dyer, Fredrick H. 141
Edington, Fowler 53
Edmiston, John 70
Edmonds, John G. 27
Edwards, Allen 27
Edwards, George 76
Edwards, James 53
Edwards, John 76
Edwards, Robert 76
Edwards, Thomas S. 76
Edwards, Timothy 28
Edwards, William 76
Eggers, John 21
Elder, Ephraim 53
Eller, Adam B. 28
Eller, Adam F. 28
Eller, Jacob 21
Eller, John W. 28

Eller, Thomas 28
Eller, William E. 28
Elliott, Stephen 21
Ellis, John E. 70
Ellison, William, Jr. 63
Elmore, William 44
England, David R. 58
Ensley, Elijah L. 46
Ensley, John 28
Epley, Andrew 37
Ervin, James M. 67
Ervin, John 67
Esteridge, Barnabas 21
Esteridge, John 21
Esteridge, William 21
Estes, Samuel 60
Estes, William 38
Evans, Henry P. 28
Evans, James L. 46
Farington, Hugh 21
Farmer, John R. 38
Farthing, John S. 67
Feagan, William J. 28
Fender, Allen 76
Fender, Wiley 76
Fender, William 76
Fisher, Jesse 28
Fisher, William 28
Flannery, Joseph 21
Fletcher, Spencer 67
Fletcher, Thomas Burt 67
Folder, John 41
Forbes, Rickler 76
Forbes, William 76
Fortune, Walter A. 58
Foster, Joseph 60
Foster, Ransom 64
Foster, Robert 28
Fowler, John M. 46
Fowler, Martin 46
Fox, Alfred 28
Fox, Alfred M. 28
Fox, Allen 28
Fox, Elbert 28

PERSONAL NAME INDEX

Fox, James M. 28
Fox, John 28
Fox, John N. 28
Fox, Lafayette 28
Fox, Melvin 28
Fox, Pinkney 28
Fox, Robert L. 28
Franklin, Andrew J. 76
Franklin, Francis M. 76
Franklin, George 76
Franklin, James 60
Franklin, John 76
Franklin, Joseph 37
Franklin, Levi A. 60
Franks, Henry 28
Franks, Joshua 28
Frazier, David C. 76
Frazier, John W. 60
Freeman, Andrew J. 28
Freeman, Benjamin F. 28
Freeman, Daniel E. 28
Freeman, George W. 28
Freeman, John A. 51
Freeman, Seth 28
Freman, David L. 54
Frisby, Lorenzo 29
Fullam, Albert W. 47
Fullbright, Miles F. 43
Galloway, Albert L. 47
Galloway, Merritt H. 47
Gardner, Thomas J. 76
Garland, Charles 60
Garland, Christopher R. 60
Garland, David 61
Garland, Elisha 61
Garland, Ezekial 61
Garland, James B. 61
Garland, John 61
Garland, John C. 76
Garland, John M. 76
Garland, Joseph E. 61
Garland, Reuben 76
Garland, Samuel 61
Garland, William J. 61

Garland, Zachariah 76
Garner, William 76
Garren, Adolphus 66
Garren, Anderson 47
Garren, Mitchell 47
Gentry, George 76
Gentry, George W. 54
Gentry, Hiram 76
Gentry, Lewis 29
Gentry, Perimeter M. 29
Gentry, Robert 54
Gentry, Thomas J. 29
Gentry, William 54, 76
Gibbs, Elias Madison 64
Gibbs, Franklin 21
Gibbs, John 64
Gibbs, Joseph A. 137
Gibbs, William 64
Gilbert, Daniel 47
Giles, James M. 63
Gillem, Alvan C. 148, 149
Gillespie, Fry B. 76
Gillespie, John 29
Gillespie, Phillip 29
Gillespie, Wilson 29
Gillis, Elbert 54
Gillon, Marcus W. 54
Gilly, George C. 21
Gilreath, Mason 47
Gladstone, Michigan 151
Glazener, Albert 29
Goforth, Ezekiel P. 54
Goforth, Miles 54
Goforth, Miles A. 58
Goings, John 63
Good, William J. 58
Gordon, James B. 132
Gosnell, Charles 54
Gosnell, James 54
Gosnell, Joeberry 54
Gosnell, Morris 54
Gosnell, Simeon 76
Goss, William 21
Gowin, Daniel H. 54

Gragg, John 67
Gragg, John S. 29
Gragg, Taylor 38
Graham, Columbus 29
Grant, 145
Graybeal, David 21
Graybeal, Reuben 21
Graybeal, William 21
Grear, Hamilton 21
Green, Athen 61
Green, George M. 64
Green, Samuel 61
Green, Starling P. 61
Green, Thomas 61
Green, Thomas S. 61
Green, William H. 38
Greene, Allen 21
Greene, Henry 38
Greene, Levi 67
Greenweld, John 21
Greer, Andrew 22
Greer, John 22
Gregory, Milas L. 54
Gregory, William M. 54
Griffin, Isaac 61
Griffin, James 37
Griffy, James 54
Griffy, William Thomas 70
Griggs, James P. 29
Grindstaff, Lawrence E. 61
Grogan, Jordan 77
Grooms, George, Jr. 45
Grooms, James 29
Grooms, John 45
Guge, Joseph L. 61
Guge, Samuel C. 61
Guinn, Jackson 45
Gunter, Jason R. 54
Gunther, Charles 54
Guthrie, John W. 29
Guthrie, Thaddeus O. 29
Guthrie, William H. 29
Hagans, Colston G. 29
Hair, Henry C. 54

Hall, George 45
Hall, George W. 29
Hall, Jesse P. 70
Hall, Leander 45
Hall, William H. 70
Hamblen, William 29
Hamilton, Hughey C. 29
Hamilton, Joseph 29
Hamilton, Robert F. 29
Hamilton, Solomon W. 47
Hamilton, Voltaire 29
Hamilton, William H. 29
Hamlet, Oliver Merritt 77
Hamlin, William 29
Hammit, James V. 47
Hammons, James 47
Hampton, Christopher C. 77
Hampton, Daniel 64
Hampton, Henry M. 77
Hampton, John 29
Hampton, Turley 29
Hampton, William F. 77
Handy, Noel 70
Handy, Thomas B. 70
Handy, William H. 70
Haney, William T. 43
Hanks, William 70
Hanner, Simpson A. 70
Hansley, A. J. 77
Harbin, David T. 45
Harbin, Oliver N. 45
Harden, George W. 44
Haren, Archibald L. 29
Haren, Judson D. 29
Harland, James 29
Harless, James 70
Harmon, Andrew J. 67
Harmon, David A. 40
Harmon, Lawson 40
Harmon, Will M. 40
Harreld, Simon 61
Harris, John A. 29
Harris, John C. 58

Harrison, Joseph E. 38
Harrison, Joseph W. 77
Harrison, Nathan 70
Hartley, James 67
Hartley, Lewis 38
Hartness, Henry L. 41
Hartness, Thomas 41
Hase, Jesse 137
Hathely, Riley B. 67
Hatley, John F. 67
Hatley, Wiley 67
Hatton, Warren A. 77
Hawkins, Jesse D. 38
Hayes, William H. 70
Haynes, Edward A. 58
Haynie, James M. 58
Haynie, John 58
Haynie, William G. 58
Hays, Joseph F. 70
Headrick, James 77
Heagin, Wilson N. 70
Heatherly, David 47
Heatherly, Merritt R. 47
Heatherly, Moses 29
Hembree, Joseph C. 29
Henderson, Benjamin F. 47
Henderson, Charles 30
Henderson, George 47
Henderson, Hensley 47
Henderson, John 54
Henderson, Leonard W. 30
Henderson, Robert B. 30
Henderson, William H. 47
Henderson, William M. 47
Henderson, Zachariah 54
Hendrow, Jesse 70
Henry, Joseph 66
Hensley, Abraham 77
Hensley, Adolphus 77
Hensley, Amos 54
Hensley, Beverly 77
Hensley, Charles W. 30
Hensley, Elijah 30

Hensley, Ephraim 77
Hensley, Ezekial 77
Hensley, George W. 77
Hensley, Goodson M. 77
Hensley, James W. 77
Hensley, Jesse 77
Hensley, John H. 77
Hensley, Klingman 77
Hensley, Logan 77
Hensley, Lorenzo 77
Hensley, Silas B. 77
Hensley, William 77
Hensley, William M. 77
Hensley, Wilson 77
Hensley, Zachariah 54
Hensly, Howell 77
Hensly, Matthew 54
Hensly, Thomas 77
Henson, Anderson 41
Henson, James 41
Henson, Matthew 54
Henson, Milton 52
Henson, William W. 51
Herron, Joshua 30
Hesterband, John 51
Heysinger, Isaac W. 142
Higgins, Gaston 78
Higgins, James Erwin 78
Higgins, James K. 78
Higgins, John 78
Higgins, Lucius 78
Higgins, William M. 78
Hildebrand, Ohio 30
Hilderman, Walter C., III 151
Hileman, John C. 61
Hill, 145
Hill, Aaron L. 54
Hill, Riley 45
Hilliard, Alfred, Jr. 67
Hilliard, James R. 22
Hilton, John W. 22
Hobbs, Calib A. 38
Hodge, Waitsel 67

Hodges, Demarcus 67
Hodges, Willry J. 67
Holcombe, Isaac 30
Holcombe, John 54
Holden, Governor 8
Hollifield, Joel A. 64
Hollifield, William H. 38
Holt, Stephen 54
Honeycutt, David 78
Honeycutt, Lafayette 78
Honeycutt, Noah 78
Honeycutt, Rubin 78
Hood, James B. 30
Hood, Perry Newton 47
Hooper, Alfred M. 51
Hooper, Henry M. 51
Hoover, Daniel 78
Hoover, Jefferson 40
Hoppes, Joseph H. 61
Hoppis, Alex 37
Hopson, William 58
Horton, Almarine H. 41
Horton, John 38
Horton, William R. 67
Houghstetler, J. B. 58
Howell, Alvin P. 22
Howell, Ancy B. 70
Howell, George W. 70
Howell, James 78
Howell, James H. 38
Howell, Jesse P. 61
Howell, John O. 70
Howell, Swinfield 61
Hoyle, Joel 44
Hudgins, Andrew J. 58
Huggins, John B. 30
Huggins, Langford 30
Huggins, Odious M. 47
Hughes, James 78
Hughes, John 61
Hughes, William J. 61
Hughey, Hamilton H. 30
Hughey, James 30
Hughey, Samuel G. 30

Hughey, William 30
Humphrey, Young 70
Hunter, Andrew J. 30
Hunter, Thomas 30
Hunter, Wiley C. 30
Hunter, William R. 30
Huntley, Isaac A. 61
Hurt, Jesse 67
Huskins, Jubal 37
Huskins, William C. 37
Hutchings, Wright 137
Ingle, Eavans 30
Ingle, Robert H. 30
Inscoe, John 113, 146
Inscoe, John C. 114
Isaac, Noah 67
Isaac, Solomon 67
Jackson, 145
Jackson, Squire P. 38
Jamison, James P. 58
Jarrett, Eli H. 78
Jaynes, Burgess G. 58
Jenkins, Francis N. 30
Jenkins, John 64
Jennings, Allen 70
Jennings, John J. 71
Jennings, Reuben 71
John, (Native American) 41
John Di-A, (Native American) 41
John-I-Got-Pa, (Native American) 41
Johnson, Allen Richard 40
Johnson, Andrew 11
Johnson, David H. 37
Johnson, Finley P. 71
Johnson, George 78
Johnson, Isaac 61
Johnson, John 71
Johnson, Stephen 41
Johnston, Joseph E. 136, 137, 140
Jolley, Milas 71
Jondon, Robert 52

Jones, A. H. 143
Jones, Alexander Hamilton 4, 6-13, 15, 114, 146
Jones, Eli 71
Jones, Hezekiah 47
Jones, Hicks 47
Jones, Hiram K. 47
Jones, Isaac C. 30
Jones, James 47, 114
Jones, John 47
Jones, Levi 114
Jones, Robert Jr. 47, 114
Jones, Robert Sr. 47, 114
Jones, Solomon 47
Jones, Thomas 47
Jones, Thomas M. 61
Jones, W. W. 114
Jones, William 64
Jordan, Weymouth T. 5, 18, 140
Justice, Joshua F. 47
Justice, Robert M. 64
Justus, James N. 30
Justus, Jesse R. 47
Justus, William R. 47
Kanot, John 41
Kanot, Tatageesga 51
Kanot, Thomas 41
Keeter, James C. 64
Keith, Caleb N. 30
Keith, James 138
Keller, Jessie R. 67
Keller, Nicholas 78
Kelly, John 64
Kennemore, Charles W. 48
Kennemore, John R. 48
Kerby, James M. 39
Kerley, Richard 30
Kilby, Samuel 71
Kilby, William 22
Kilby, William J. 71
Killian, John C. 78
Kilpatrick, William P. 48
King, James 22

King, Martin A. 30
Kirk, 151
Kirk, George W. 10, 148
Kirkendall, Ezekiel 48
Kirkendall, Isaac 30
Kirkendall, John F. 63
Kirkendall, Joseph 48
Kirkendall, Thomas M. 30
Kiser, Robert G. 44
Kitchen, Jason 48
Kite, Russell 61
Knight, George W. 52
Knight, John L. 52
Konk-as-ke, (Native American) 41
Kuykendall, Alfred 48
Kuykendall, Jahew (John) 30
Landers, Beverly 78
Landers, Tilman H. 78
Lane, Benjamin 71
Lane, Jacob 37
Lankford, William J. 31
Lanning, Andrew J. 48, 66
Lanning, William C. 48
Laughter, Elias 63
Laws, Andrew J. 71
Laws, Daniel P. 71
Laws, David 71
Laws, David S. 71
Laws, James B. 78
Laws, James W. 78
Laws, John M. 78
Laws, Rufus 71
Leadford, Center 41
Leadford, Elisha M. 41
Leadford, James L. 41
Leadford, Jason 41
Leadford, Julius 41
Leakey, John S. 59
Leaky, Henry 59
Ledbetter, Philo 66
Ledbetter, Thomas B. 63

Ledford, Christopher C. 137
Ledford, David 41
Ledford, James H. 78
Ledford, Joseph 31
Ledford, Joseph S. 31
Ledford, Obidiah 31
Ledford, Thomas 61
Ledford, William C. 41
Lee, Robert E. 1, 2, 129, 140, 147
Leveritt, Jesse L. 48
Lewis, Alexander 22
Lewis, James 22, 67
Lewis, James W. 78
Lewis, Joseph 54
Lewis, Matthew A. 78
Lewis, Robert 31
Lincoln, 3, 9, 135, 150, 151
Linden, Adolphus 71
Lindsey, Thomas 31
Lineback, Henry 61
Lippord, Lewis 71
Livingston, John 71
Lockaby, George W. 31
Loftis, Elijah N. 66
Loftis, Frederick F. 66
Lofton, Harison A. 48
Loftus, John H. 37
Loftus, Kosea D. 48
Long, William 44
Loudermilk, John L. 54
Louis H. Manarin 5
Love, William N. 52
Lunsford, David 31
Lunsford, Eli 31
Lunsford, Ephraim 31
Lunsford, Henry 31
Lunsford, James 31
Lunsford, Jeremiah 31
Lunsford, Levi 31
Mace, Solomon 78
Man, Andrew 45
Manarin, Louis H. 18, 140

Mann, William 31
Marlow, Harvey 71
Marrow, Harrison 64
Marshal, Thomas 48
Martin, Albert 45
Martin, James P. 44
Massey, Andrew J. 31
Massey, Jefferson 31
Massey, Samuel 31
Masters, Abraham 78
Matheson, John 68
Matthews, Henry Calvin 59
McCall, Alexander G. 48
McCall, John A. 48
McCall, Samuel 66
McClain, Rufus T. 48
McClean, Sidney 78
McCloud, David F. 68
McCourry, Oliver 78
McCoury, James 78
McCoury, James O. 78
McCoury, Tilman H. 79
McCoury, Zephaniah 79
McCoy, Daniel M. 59
McCoy, Hiram 22
McCoy, Peter 79
McCoy, William 71
McCoy, William J. 54
McCracken, John 79
McCracken, William H. 45
McCrary, Adolphus 48
McDowell, 134
McDowell, Charles L. 79
McDowell, George M. 79
McFall, Abraham 37
McFalls, Daniel 31
McFalls, George F. 137
McGaha, Joseph 31
McGaha, William H. 48
McGalliard, William H. 61
McGee, James F. 41
McGee, James H. 68

PERSONAL NAME INDEX

McGlammon, 71
McGlumley, 71
McGuire, James 62
McIntire, Zachary 45
McIntosh, John 79
McInturff, Clayton 79
McKinney, Gordon 146
McKinney, John 31, 62
McKinney, Samuel 79
McKinney, Waitstel 59
McLean, Woodfin K. 55
McMahan, Charles B. 79
McMahan, David A. 79
McMahan, Edward 79
McMahan, John Y. 79
McMahon, Archibald B. 79
McMahon, George 79
McMahon, James 79
McMahon, William B. 79
McMurray, Andrew W. 65
McMurray, William G. 65
McNeal, Alexander 79
McNeal, Archibald 79
McNeal, John 79
McPeters, Jonathan 79
Medcalf, John 79
Melton, Lewis E. 31
Merrell, Perry 48
Merrell, Samuel 48
Merrell, William F. 48
Merrill, A. B. 22
Metcalf, Levi 55
Metcalf, William 55
Michael, Creed 22
Michael, Frederick 22
Michael, Lorenzo D. 22
Miller, Columbus 71
Miller, Hiram 79
Miller, Jacob 79
Miller, James L. 22
Miller, Jesse M. 68
Miller, John 68, 79
Miller, John H. 31
Miller, John K. 149

Miller, Marcus 68
Miller, Samuel 52, 79
Miller, Timothy 79
Minton, Pervis 71
Mitchell, Berry 37
Moody, Benjamin 68
Moody, Edward C. 68
Moody, Francis 39
Moody, William H. 59
Moore, 85
Moore, Hezekiah P. 48
Moore, J. F. 55
Moore, John W. 88
Moore, Riley L. 71
Moore, William R. 48
Morgan, James N. 31
Morgan, Pinkney A. 37
Morrison, David M. 48
Morrison, James 79
Morrow, G. W. 63
Moses, David 43
Moss, William 79
Mull, Henry 37
Mull, Leander 45
Mull, William E. 45
Munson, Pierce R. 31
Munson, Robert S. 31
Neal, J. Marion 44
Neasbill, Thomas L. 59
Nelson, Elisha K. 48
Newton, Alvin 22
Nichols, Abraham 71
Nichols, Alexander H. 52
Nichols, Gilbert R. 52
Nichols, Henry H. 71
Nicholson, Lazarus 71
Noppen, Van 151
Norman, Joseph T. 71
Norris, Jesse F. 71
Norton, Balis 79
Norton, David 80
Norton, George, Jr. 55
Norton, George, Sr. 55
Norton, Hackney 55

Norton, James 55
Norton, Jesse 80
Norton, John 55
Norton, Josiah 55
Norton, Martin 55, 80
Norton, Morris 55
Norton, Roderick 80
Norton, William 55, 80
Norton, William, Jr. 55
Nuves, Henry 22
Oaks, Jeremiah 62
Oaks, Nehemiah 62
Odear, William H. 59
Ogle, William B. 80
Ok-Wa-Taga, (Native American) 51
Oliver, John C. 52
Oliver, Madison C. 52
Oliver, Resa 31
Oliver, William P. 52
Only, Robert H. 65
Ool-Ay-Way, Thomas (Native American) 51
Ool-Stoo-Ee, John (Native American) 51
Orr, Caleb 31
Orr, George L. 48
Orr, Robert F. 48
Osborn, Aris 22
Osborn, Jeremiah 22
Osborne, David 22
Osteen, Calvin 48
Osteen, Elijah 31
Osteen, Elisha 31
Osteen, John C. 48
Osteen, Luke 48
Osteen, Richard S. 49
Osteen, Robert V. 49
Osteen, Solomon D. 49
Oter, James (Native American) 41
Oter, Thomas (Native American) 51
Owen, Butler 142

Owens, Alexander 51
Owens, John A. 49
Pace, William J. 49
Pack, George W. 31
Paine, Daniel 32
Paine, Isaiah 32
Paine, James 32
Paine, John H. 32
Palle, David (Native American) 41
Palmer, John A. 32
Palmer, Joseph M. 39
Palmer, William J. 149
Pane, James 32
Pannel, William T. 32
Panther, John 32
Pardew, Abner 71
Pardue, Joel 71
Paris, Henry 49
Paris, Jackson 32
Paris, Levi 55
Parker, Carson 65
Parker, John F. 32
Parker, Thomas M. 32
Partridge, Chur (Native American) 51
Partridge, Colsgun (Native American) 51
Patterson, Calloway 62
Patterson, Drewry W. 49
Patterson, Luther C. 65
Patterson, William 32
Patterson, William A. 42
Patton, Robert 32
Patton, William L. 49
Payne, 145
Payne, Adolphus M. 55
Payne, Isaiah 32
Payne, James 55
Payne, James M. 14, 32
Payne, James O. 52
Payne, Melinda Reeves 14
Payne, Robert 14
Payne, Zebulon 72

Pearce, Redmond T. 39
Pearson, Adolphus A. 49
Peek, Garrett 32
Peek, William Henry 32
Pendland, Robert B. 32
Pendley, Sidney E. 39
Pendley, Silas J. 39
Penland, Charles A. 80
Penland, Hiram 45
Penland, James R. 32
Penland, Jesse 80
Pennington, William 22
Perdue, Joseph H. 72
Perry, William D. 32
Petersen, Lawson 80
Petersen, Moses 80
Petersen, Moses Jr. 80
Petersen, Ruben 80
Petersen, Samuel 80
Phillips, Columbus 22
Phillips, Guthridge K. 62
Phillips, Hugh 72
Phillips, William 22, 80
Phillips, William J. 80
Philyan, Gideon 39
Phipps, Jacob N. 80
Pickens, John C. 32
Pickens, Robert H. 32
Pinion, Andrew 55
Pitman, Reuben 62
Plemmons, Adolphus H., Jr. 42
Ponder, Robert 55
Porter, James M. 72
Porter, William F. 72
Powers, John 32
Prather, Amos 65
Prestwood, Luther M. 39
Price, Isaiah 72
Pritchard, Adolphus 37
Proctor, James 52
Proctor, Reuben 62
Pryor, Robert Pinkney 44
Queen, Finley A. 72

Queen, Pickney H. 72
Queen, Robert T. 45
Queen, Samuel R. 72
Queen, William R. 72
Quinn, Joseph 59
Radford, Samuel F. 80
Raines, Nathan 63
Ramsey, George 55
Ramsey, Jackson 32
Ramsey, James 32, 55
Ramsey, Jobe 32
Ramsey, John 80
Ramsey, Joseph R. 80
Ramsey, Lewis W. 32
Ramsey, Robert 32
Ramsey, William W. 32
Randal, James 137
Randall, James Mitchell 55
Randall, John B. 32
Rash, Lindsay 68
Rash, Martin 32
Rash, Thomas J. 72
Ratcliff, Mason 42
Rathbone, Henry C. 80
Ravel, Henry B. 44
Ray, Albert 80
Ray, Barnett 80
Ray, Hiram 80
Ray, James A. 80
Ray, James H. 55
Ray, James M. 80
Ray, John H. 80
Ray, Joseph 42
Ray, Leander 80
Ray, Nathan M. 80
Ray, Samuel B. 80
Ray, Samuel P. 80
Ray, Thomas 33
Ray, Thomas E. 80
Ray, William H. 81
Ray, William S. 55
Rector, Alfred 33
Rector, Elijah 55
Rector, Enoch 33

Rector, Franklin 33
Rector, Julius 33
Rector, Samuel 33
Rector, William C. 55
Redman, David 55
Reece, Hugh 72
Reece, John 68
Reese, Alson E. 49
Reese, Martin V. 33
Reese, Patterson 33
Reese, William R. 33
Renfrow, Thomas 81
Revis, Alford Goodson 33
Revis, Henry M. 33
Revis, Jacob M. 33
Revis, Thomas H. 33
Rhoads, John A. 72
Rhoads, William D. 72
Rhodes, Benjamin 72
Rice, Albert 81
Rice, Edmund 55
Rice, Hiram 81
Rice, Isaac 55
Rice, James 55
Rice, James M. 55
Rice, Job 33
Rice, Joseph L. 33
Rice, Spencer 33
Rice, Stephen 81
Rice, Thomas 56
Rice, Thomas J. 81
Rice, Thomas Shephard 56
Rice, Wesley 33
Rich, William 65
Richardson, Moses F. 72
Riddle, Hezekiah 56
Riddle, Hiram B. 81
Riddle, James E. 81
Riddle, James M. 62
Riddle, John 81
Riddle, Marvill 81
Riddle, Nathan 81
Riddle, William M. 81
Ridons, James 56

Rigsbee, William 56
Roach, Newton 65
Roalten, William 22
Roark, Alfred W. 22
Roark, Ephram 22
Robbins, James 22
Roberson, Richard, Sr. 45
Roberson, Young 81
Roberts, Alfred 56
Roberts, Andrew J. 33
Roberts, Davis 56
Roberts, Elisha 45
Roberts, George 33
Roberts, George M. 33
Roberts, George W. 33
Roberts, Henry C. 33
Roberts, Jacob M. 52
Roberts, John 33
Roberts, John J. 33
Roberts, John P. 33
Roberts, Martin L. 56
Roberts, Ninevah 33
Roberts, Robert K. 33
Roberts, Stephen 33
Roberts, William 45
Roberts, William R. 33
Roberts, Wyley S. 33
Roberts, Zeb B. 56
Robertson, General M. 65
Robertson, Greenberry 81
Robertson, James I., Jr. 140
Robertson, Samuel C. 56
Robinson, Mitchell E. 56
Roebling, Washington 88
Rogers, Jasper 33
Rogers, Perry 34
Rogers, William 34
Roland, George W. 81
Roland, James W. 43
Roller, Reuben 22
Rollins, Isaac 49
Rollins, William W. 56
Rose, Wyatt 22
Rotan, Jacob 22

Rotan, John 72
Runnion, Thomas I. 56
Russell, John P. 72
Russell, Noah 72
Sames, Edward 56
Sams, Anson 34
Sams, Asa W. 56
Sams, Ezekial 81
Sams, Gabriel 56
Sams, James R. 56
Sams, Robert B. 81
Sams, William Washington 56
Sams, Zephaniah 34
Sanders, Alexander 22
Sanders, David 72
Sanders, J. S. 56
Sawyer, Archibald 34
Sawyer, Lewis S. 34
Scott, Lorenzo D. 62
Scott, Samuel W. 151
Scroggins, James O. 65
Scroggins, John N. 65
Searcy, David W. 66
Searcy, Elijah J. 66
Searcy, Samuel D. 65
Searcy, William B. 65
Seay, James M. 51
Sebastine, Lewis W. 72
Sentell, Guilford 34
Sentell, James L. 34
Sentell, Jesse B. 34
Sentell, John E. 34
Sentell, William R. 34
Setser, John H. 39
Sexton, Elijah 65
Shehan, Bynum 49
Shehan, James E. 59
Shehan, John 49
Shelton, Andrew J. 56
Shelton, Christopher C. 56
Shelton, Clingman 56
Shelton, David 56
Shelton, David Jr. 81

Shelton, David Sr. 81
Shelton, Elifuse 56
Shelton, Eliphus 56
Shelton, George 81
Shelton, Isaac 56
Shelton, James 56
Shelton, John 81
Shelton, Roderick 34
Shelton, William 81
Sheppard, John W. 81
Sheppard, Mitchell G. 81
Sheppard, Thomas E. 81
Sherrill, C. Elisha 39
Sherrill, Joseph H. 40
Shinolt, Calvin 81
Shipman, Alexander 49
Shipman, Alexander F. 34
Shipman, Caleb 49
Shipman, Edmond C. 49
Shipman, Edward 34
Shipman, Francis A. 49
Shipman, James S. 34
Shipman, John B. 49
Shipman, John M. 34
Shipman, Marion P. 49
Shipman, William 49
Shores, James C. 72
Shumate, Enoch C. 72
Shumate, Mark H. 72
Shumate, Wesley 72
Simes, John L. 65
Simmons, Henry C. 72
Simmons, Leander 59
Simms, James 39
Simpson, Merritt R. 66
Sims, Owenby 34
Skitta, Mike 51
Slu-Na-Na, (Native American) 42
Sluder, Felix 23
Sluder, James C. 34
Small, Jesse 39
Small, Kelly 39
Smith, 134

Smith, Francis 68
Smith, John 65
Smith, John E. 49
Smith, John H. 40
Smith, Ransom 37
Smith, William 59
Smith, William S. 59
Snelson, William R. 34
Snider, Henry J. 34
South, George 23
Spain, James M. 49
Sparks, Elijah 72
Sparks, Ervin 81
Sparks, James 62
Sparks, Lewis M. 62
Sparks, Whitfield 62
Spigner, William 68
Sprinkle, David 34
Sprinkle, George 34
Sprinkle, Humphrey 34
Sprinkle, James 34
Sprinkle, Michael 34
Sprinkle, Obadiah 72
Sprinkle, William S. 34
Squirrel, Souquilla (Native American) 42
Stamey, Jacob H. 43
Stamey, Martin V. 37
Stanfield, Thomas L. 52
Stanly, William H. 34
Stansberry, Solomon 37
Stanton, John 81
Stanton, William 39
Staton, Jesse A. 49
Stepp, Abraham T. 49
Stepp, Alfred 49
Stepp, Henry 34
Stepp, Reuben M. 49
Stepp, Robert 49
Stepp, William H. 49
Steward, Melvin M. 49
Stewart, Joseph S. 62
Stewart, Thomas 49
Stewman, Thomas 34

Stills, George M. 34
Stines, George N. 34
Stines, Joseph E. 35
Stockton, Francis M. 56
Stoneman, 148, 151
Story, Noah 23
Stout, Andrew 37
Stout, Thomas 62
Stout, William 62
Stradley, Ebenezer W. 35
Street, Charles 62
Street, John D. 62
Street, Stephen 62
Street, William H. 62
Strickland, William 68
Stringfield, William 125
Sullivan, Johnathan 35
Suttles, Joseph 35
Sutton, John 51
Swafford, James 44
Swaney, Isham H. 49
Swanger, George W. 52
Swangim, John 50
Swangim, William N. 35
Swangin, John B. 50
Swangin, Thomas 66
Sylvers, James 81
Tabor, Govan 35
Tah-Li, (Native American) 42
Taylor, Eli 23
Taylor, James M. 65
Taylor, Jeremiah 50
Taylor, Jeremiah M. 50
Taylor, John 56
Taylor, John D. 50
Taylor, John W. 81
Taylor, Obediah 63
Taylor, Samuel J. 35
Te-Ke-How-Gous-Ki, (Native American) 42
Teague, Edward 57
Teague, James I. 39
Teague, Nathan A. 39

Tenison, William P. 63
Thomas, David 81
Thomas, Hezekiah 17, 19, 68
Thomas, John 35
Thomas, Peter 57
Thomas, William Holland 123, 125
Thompson, James M. 82
Thompson, John H. 39
Thompson, Joseph 82
Tipton, Alfred D. 82
Tipton, Charles 82
Tipton, David 42
Tipton, David P. 82
Tipton, John D. 82
Tipton, Jonathan 82
Tipton, Samuel 82
Tipton, Sanders H. 82
Tipton, Sebron 82
Tipton, Valentine 82
Tipton, Wiley 82
Tipton, William 82
Tomlinson, Hiram 23
Tompkins, Steven 82
Tow, Samuel M. 50
Tow, Shaderack 35
Townsend, John G. 35
Townsend, Robert 51
Trantham, Merritt C. 35
Treadway, James 35
Treadway, John 35
Triplet, Darby 68
Triplet, Elbert G. 72
Triplet, Moses 68
Triplet, Thomas H. 72
Triplett, Elbert 72
Triplett, Sidney 73
Triplett, Thomas 73
Triplett, William 73
Trotter, William R. 140
Trull, William A. 42
Tucker, Calvin 68
Turner, Elijah W. 65

Tweed, Albert 35
Twiggs, John 65
Tyre, Thomas M. 73
Vance, Zeb 12, 113
Vance, Zebulon Baird 119
Vanover, Ripley 23
Vess, David M. 45
Vess, Zephaniah 65
Vi-Na-Der, (Native American) 42
Vick, Robert C. 35
Vincent, Tom 115, 117
Voncannon, Abram B. 73
Waddell, Russel 57
Waddell, Samuel 57
Wade, William 40
Wadkins, John 51
Waggoner, Adam 35
Wai-Le, (Native American) 42
Waldrop, John 35
Waldrop, William 57
Walker, Ishan 23
Walker, James 73
Walker, James W. 73
Walker, John 42
Walker, John A. 73
Walker, Jonathan C. 59
Walker, Robert 73
Walker, Robert D. 50
Walker, Thomas E. 65
Walker, William 65
Walkingstick, James (Native American) 51
Walkingstick, Thomas (Native American) 51
Walkins, John W. 73
Wallace, Samuel 73
Ward, John 35
Ward, Michael 137
Ward, William N. 35
Washington, (Native American) 42
Watkins, Andrew 73

Watson, Henry Eli 39
Watson, Melton 73
Watson, Noah 39
Watson, Tilingham H. 39
Watson, William 73
Watts, Manly C. 39
Watts, Rufus 50
Watts, William 57, 59
Waycaster, Stephen 37
Webb, John Calvin 39
Webb, Joseph M. 82
Weese, John 50
Weese, William 35
Welch, Bennett H. 82
Welch, Sydney 82
West, Albert S. 63
West, Andrew Jackson 35
West, George W. 35
West, John 35
West, John P. 35
West, Leonard 35
West, Marcus 35
West, William B. 35
West, William L. 57
West, William P. 35
West, Zachariah 57
Wheeler, Hiram N. 82
Wheeler, James M. 82
Wheeler, John H. 82
Whitaker, Solomon 35
White, Ambrose 68
White, Henry A. 35
White, James 35
White, Jefferson 36
White, Joseph H. 39
White, Leander 23
White, Pharoah 36
White, William 36
Whitmore, Columbus C. 36
Whitson, Isaac 82
Whitson, Madison 82
Wilborn, James M. 73
Wilds, Jacob H. 57

Wilds, John H. 36
Wilds, John M. 57
Wilds, Robert 36
Williams, John H. 36
Williams, Robert P. 45
Williams, Silas 82
Williams, Thomas 23, 62
Williams, William 82
Willis, John A. 57, 82
Willson, Michael 57
Wilson, Edward 82
Wilson, Harrison 36
Wilson, James 42
Wilson, James M. 82
Wilson, Jesse N. 65
Wilson, John 82
Wilson, John C. 82
Wilson, Levi 82
Wilson, Marion 68
Wilson, Thomas J. 82
Wilson, William 83
Wilson, William B. 83
Wilson, William F. 37
Woestemeyer, Ina 151
Wolf, Elbert S. 36
Wood, John B. 51
Wood, William J. 51
Wood, William M. 73
Woodring, David C. 51
Woodson, Francis Marion 36
Woody, Green 36
Wooten, Thomas K. F. 43
Worley, Henry 57
Worley, Joseph D. 36
Worley, Wiley G. 83
Worley, Wiley J. 36
Wright, James M. 36
Wright, John W. 57
Wright, Leander 36
Wright, Monteville 36
Wright, Thomas J. 36
Wright, William T. 36
Wy-An-Is-Te, (Native American) 42
Wyatt, Alfred J. 36
Wyatt, Victory 73
Yates, Alfred 73
Yeates, Jesse F. 73
Yeates, John D. 73
Yelton, James 73
You-Lak-Da, (Native American) 42
Younce, Elijah 23
Younce, George 73
Young, Alford 83
Young, Clinton E. 57
Young, James W. 83
Young, Lynch 36
Young, Merritt 62
Young, Strobridge 62
Young, Wilson 62
Youngblood, Hiram 137
Younger, Joseph 73
Younger, William G. 73
Younts, E. F. 137

Place Name Index

Andersonville 87
Appalachia 146
Ashe County 4, 20, 21, 88, 89, 90
Asheville 11, 143
Asheville 143
Asheville, North Carolina 12, 118, 119, 134
Avery County 4
Bloody Madison 138
Boone, North Carolina 14, 151
Buncombe County 4, 20, 24, 89, 91, 118, 119, 134, 146
Burke County 4, 20, 37, 89, 93, 120
Caldwell County 4, 20, 38, 89, 94, 121
California 11
Camp Douglas 19
Camp Vance 148
Castle Thunder Prison 6
Catawba County 4, 20, 40, 89, 95, 113, 122
Cherokee County 4, 20, 41, 89, 96, 128
Cherokee Reservation 123
Cherokee, North Carolina 123
Cherokees 102
Chicago, Illinois 19
Clay County 4, 20, 43, 89, 97, 128
Cleveland County 5, 20, 44, 89, 98, 113, 124
Cocke County, Tennessee 10
Confederate Conscription Act 135
Cumberland Gap 147
Dalton, Georgia 136, 140

Des Moines, Iowa 143
Dixie Highway 129
Etowah Branch, Henderson County Library 133
Etowah, North Carolina 133
Fort Gregg 88
Fort Kerney, Nebraska 19
Fort Sumter 3, 9, 135
Franklin, North Carolina 128
Frazier Farm 135
Fredericksburg 135
Gains Mill 135
Gatlin 88
Georgia 87
Gettysburg 3, 86, 135
Goldsboro, North Carolina 115, 117
Graham County 4
Grand Island, Nebraska 19
Greenhill Cemetery, Waynesville, North Carolina 125
Haversack 140
Haywood County 5, 20, 45, 89, 99, 125
Henderson County 5, 20, 46, 89, 100, 114, 116, 126, 133, 142, 144-146, 151
Henderson County Library, Etowah Branch 133
Hendersonville, North Carolina 114, 126, 143, 146
Hickory, North Carolina 151

Jackson County 4, 5, 20, 51, 89, 101, 127
Jonesborough, Georgia 19
Knoxville, Tennessee 114, 149
Lenoir, North Carolina 121
Long Beach, California 11
Louisville, Kentucky 19
Macon County 4, 5, 20, 52, 89, 102, 128
Madison County 5, 14, 15, 20, 53, 89, 103, 129, 137
Malvern Hill 135
Marshall, North Carolina 129, 137
Maryland 11, 142
McDowell County 5, 20, 58, 89, 104
Mitchell County 5, 20, 60, 89, 105, 150
Morganton, North Carolina 120, 148
Morristown, Tennessee 151
Nashville, Tennessee 19
Newton, North Carolina 122
Northern Virginia 147
Oklahoma 11
Old Wilkes Jail 131
Pearl Harbor 3
Pennsylvania 149
Petersburg 88
Philadelphia, Pennsylvania 151
Polk County 5, 20, 63, 89, 106, 113
Raleigh 88
Raleigh, North Carolina 88, 117, 140, 151
Richmond, Virginia 6
Rowan County 16
Rutherford County 5, 20, 64, 89, 107, 113, 130
Rutherfordton, North Carolina 130
Saint Paul's Episcopal Church cemetery 132
Shelby, North Carolina 124
Shelton Laurel 137-139, 148
Shelton Laurel Creek 139
Smith-McDowell House 134
Spartanburg, South Carolina 151
Swain County 4
Sylva, North Carolina 127
Tennessee 5, 8, 15, 16, 136, 138, 140, 149, 150
Transylvania County 5, 20, 66, 89, 108
Virginia 18
Washington, D.C. 11-13, 143, 151
Watauga County 5, 19, 20, 67, 89, 109
Waynesville, North Carolina 125
Wilkes County 4-5, 7, 20, 69, 89, 110, 117, 131-132, 147
Wilkesboro, North Carolina 131, 132
Winston-Salem, North Carolina 140
Yancey County 5, 20, 74, 89, 111